Spotlight on the

Art of

The Story

I0161308

Edited By:

Rebecca Fegan

Contributors:

Janel Asche ▪ Mark Fegan ▪

Rebecca Fegan ▪Angie Garfield ▪ Christine Jones

Keith Jones ▪ Evelyn Mosley ▪ Randy Prier

Spotlight on the Art of The Story

Contributors:

Janel Asche, Mark Fegan, Rebecca Fegan, Angie Garfield,

Christine Jones, Keith Jones, Evelyn Mosley, Randy Prier

Copyright © 2024 Alternative Book Club.

All rights reserved.

Published by Keith Jones / Kitewind LLC

ISBN **978-1-964649-01-6**

Edited by Rebecca Fegan

Cover Design by Keith Jones, alternativebookclub.com.

Printed and bound in the United States of America.

First Edition

Preface

Stories carry our heritage and history, teach us, spark imagination, and inspire growth. They hook us in video games, linger from campfire tales, and keep us reading late into the night. Stories are billion-dollar industries—movies, TV shows, comedy, video games, music, books, keynote speaking, and social media—drawing people out of their homes to communal viewing spaces and prompting them to purchase and repeatedly watch these narratives.

Beloved stories begin with phrases like "The kingdom of heaven is like...", "Once upon a time...", "Back in the time when tigers smoked...", or "A long time ago in a galaxy far, far away...". They resonate because they touch familiar feelings, whether comforting, frightening, or chaotic.

I love stories! They connect me to my family history, expand my imagination, and inspire me to contribute to my own story. For instance, our family has a story about my great-grandfather, a Lutheran pastor who came to Nebraska in the early 1800s. He established Lutheran churches and, feeling called back to Germany, left despite his wife's protest. He died on the voyage and was buried at sea. When one of his churches celebrated its

125th anniversary, we were invited as descendants, and seeing the story in print sparked my passion for collecting family stories.

The Alternative Book Club has a dynamic and collaborative approach to creating writing projects. With the input from various perspectives—my son's LARP world-building insights and my daughter's idea of character sheets, the "Art of the Story" seemed like a fascinating title. As the editor, it became my job to weave together diverse contributions and shape them into a unified narrative.

Collaborative writing posed challenges, such as determining a starting point. Each chapter could logically be the first, so we decided you could start reading anywhere. We aimed to provide tools for both written and oral stories, useful in various contexts like speeches, social media posts, blogs, and oral traditions.

This book cannot in any way be considered exhaustive coverage of such a large topic, but we hope to bring some clarity and provide a step in the right direction.

Through our research, we've gained extensive knowledge, shared weekly in our meetings, enriching our understanding of storytelling. The Alternative Book Club fosters an intellectually and emotionally creative atmosphere, and our meetings are a highlight of my week.

This book reveals some of the secrets to crafting and presenting good stories, which can be used to teach, warn, entertain, and inspire future generations, just as our ancestors did.

I thank my children, Ben Fegan and Jo Emanuelson, for their inspiration and input.

Rebecca Fegan, editor

Spotlight on the Art of The Story

Contents

The Main Aspects

If you didn't read the Preface, *shame on you! Just kidding!* This book was put together in an unusual way. Normally we would progress logically through the different topics you need to understand. It occurred to us (this is the "royal us" normally reserved for the King and his court, but also for the supreme editor in this case) that many who are reading this book have been telling stories for a long time and have a background of speaking or writing to an audience.

As such, we have dispensed with the traditional chapter numbers and have just gone with the titles, dividing them into their component parts.

The first part will discuss the makings of a good story and why we want to craft our stories to be memorable, purposeful, and timely.

The second part will focus on some of the elements we use to make a good story to bring the characters to life and the meanings clear.

SPOTLIGHT ON THE ART OF THE STORY

The last part will be the techniques we use to focus on the message and select stories or recall stories that relate to the point we wish to make.

Do Tell!

By: Angie Garfield

"Begin your best self-discovery by telling your story"

~ Angie Garfield

Self-Discovery Through Storytelling

Self-discovery is certainly a part of storytelling. When we share our life experiences with others through storytelling, we find a piece of ourselves. It's about paying attention to how you are telling your story and thinking "How are others perceiving what I am talking about?" This world is chock-full of people who just won't ask what you are talking about. They are too polite, or they don't want to hurt your feelings if they ask, or they simply don't care and just want you to stop talking! I have told stories to all these polite listeners. Believe me, I am forever grateful for them. I remember feeling bad at times though, thinking "Why didn't they stop me?"

Not long ago, I went to a get-together with some friends of mine. I thought to myself, "I am so glad I was invited to this party. I haven't seen some of these people for years!" As I walked around the room I was met with friendly faces and polite

1

greetings. The food was amazing, all finger food that included some of my favorites. I mingled for a while and had great 'catch-up' conversations. After a while, I started thinking how strange it was when you don't see people for a while, and the catch-up stories last about five to eight minutes. I chuckled to myself thinking that my life in the last few years can be compacted into about eight minutes, really? Is my life really that simple? Boring? Or is it that easy to share my life 'highlights?' I smiled and thought maybe I was just good at summarizing things that have happened to me.

I made my way through the party and took a seat next to Bill. He greeted me with a half hug and asked how I was. Bill is just a very friendly person. We were on the same sand volleyball team a long time ago. He introduced me to the people he was sitting with (five in the group). They were talking about golf. I love golf so I was very happy I sat with them. Well, I was happy for a short time. Unknowingly, Bill was telling his story about walking into a family of skunks while playing on a local golf course. I thought "Oh no. I've heard this story about five times." As he began to tell the story, it seemed it would be funny but unfortunately, it was not. The story took much longer than it should have, and every time I heard it, it was a little different. There was one thing that was the same about the story…it was longer every single time he told it. I thought "Wouldn't be a great Superpower that if, when we sat down with someone, we knew what was going to be said, we could leave in a flash?"

Could I leave? No, I was in the 'bummer bubble'. It happens when you are bummed that you must stay in a storytelling bubble you can't pop. Why? Because it's just plain impolite to pop the bummer bubble.

As Bill began to tell the story, I noticed everyone's eyes getting larger, they were all smiling, and they were in anticipation of this interesting and funny story. Slowly as Bill told the story, body language changed. These are things one observes when trapped in "the bummer bubble."

Most people are very nice when listening to someone tell a story. Mostly because the person telling the story is very nice, like Bill. I watched as some people began to look elsewhere, others would nod when they weren't supposed to, and some smiling much less. Yes, the bummer bubble was in full effect. Why couldn't Bill understand that the group wanted out of the bubble? I was polite and stayed the course, as did everyone else. At the end of the story, there was a general giggle, and everyone was smiling. I remembered the last time I heard Bill tell the story, it ended with the same reaction. I thought why would he continue to tell that story with such a low energy reaction? Perhaps he didn't understand the reaction or maybe he simply liked talking about skunks. Who knew?

Keep in mind, storytelling is a powerful social connection.

One of my self-discoveries in storytelling is that I tend to repeat the same story over to the same person. And those polite people will give their time away to me for free. I remember my sister being quieter than usual as I was telling her something that happened to me on vacation. At the end of the hilarious story, she gave a short chuckle. I asked, "Don't you think that's funny?" She said, "Yes, it's totally funny but you already told me the story." I asked, "Why didn't you stop me?" She said, "Because I think it's a funny story and I didn't mind hearing it again." I laughed thinking that was very kind. Now I tend to say, "Let me know if I told you this story already."

All in all, telling a story is a wonderful way to test the waters of your emotional intelligence. Having high emotional intelligence is key to both business and personal success. Emotional intelligence (also known as E.Q.) simply means you are in control of your emotions, as well as observing and understanding the emotions of others. Using your E.Q., you can understand if your story is affecting others in the way you intend, or if you need to wrap it up.

I found my E.Q. in storytelling to be invaluable for selling. When talking with prospective clients and telling them success stories of the product, most of the time I could tell if they were intrigued, bored, or wanted to ask questions. I used what I'd learned in self-discovery in pacing my speech, self-awareness, and just how invaluable emotional intelligence is to all communication.

Storytelling is an important part of strengthening emotional intelligence. Storytelling can be an effective way to monitor and control emotions. Also, being aware of how others perceive the message of your story, to 'read the room' and adjust to inform, motivate, or inspire.

Stronger emotional intelligence can also be attained by journaling. Journaling helps bring clarity and self-awareness, it can help to process emotions, and it is a wonderful source for self-reflection.

Journaling

When I was working full-time, I attended many seminars. I took away something meaningful from almost every seminar I attended. One seminar discussed journaling. The speaker suggested at the end of each day, journal ten things that day you were grateful for that day. When I began to journal what I was grateful for, it was effortless. As time went by became a little tougher. Then I thought to myself, who cares if I repeat what I'm grateful for every day, it's my journal!

After a few months of listing what I was grateful for, I began writing stories. Yes, journaling is storytelling. I have found writing down my thoughts is a sense of peace for me. It helps me to organize my emotions, find my psyche, and listen to my spirit. Writing down my story puts things in perspective.

I wrote about successes that I had at work. Sometimes I wrote about the challenging days, but I would go back a few pages to the successful day and would feel so much better. Journaling made me less stressed reading about how I handled certain situations. After a few days of journaling, I would take a break or even go back to listing what I was grateful for. It was fun to go back and look at my lists from months ago. I remember laughing out loud when I read one of the things on my list was – "Caught all green lights on the way to work!" Yes, it is the little things!

Journaling can be a way to get inside your world, even for a short time. And while you are there, you can explore all the amazing ways you are living your life. You discover that perhaps challenges in your life are lessons. That seems a little cliché but it is very true. Things get clarity when written down. Seeing your thoughts in words can be eye-opening!

Storytelling and self-esteem

The most significant way I found healthy self-esteem is the use of storytelling in Toastmasters. The meetings were at work, once a week over lunchtime. In my opinion, there is no better way to walk a path to healthy self-esteem than to try your best at public speaking in front of a group of your peers and tell a story. The Toastmasters group doesn't judge, well they do evaluate with the program criteria, but it is designed to help one become a better speaker. When others assure you of your talents, and let you know your communication shortcomings aren't so bad, it is a blessing.

I was able to communicate with more clarity through Toastmasters. It was wonderful to speak for a few minutes in front of a group of people and at the end, everyone clapped! How great is that? That reminds me of one of my favorite outcomes after joining Toastmasters - when my boss would tell me "I'm very busy, I'll give you five minutes" ...no problem!

Encouraging Others

I once read that every person is like a book, and if you are fortunate enough, they may let you turn a page or two and read a fascinating story.

One of my favorite parts of communicating is learning about others. I own a company, Customer First Success. I facilitate a customer service program that I designed. Throughout the facilitation, I ask participants to share more about themselves. I truly enjoy asking them about their hobbies, interests, etc.

While facilitating, I find that sharing a story, for some, is very difficult. I try my best to let people understand they are in a 'safe zone.' That means we never share what is being said outside of the class. I ask the class to respect others in the safe zone, and to this day, that request has been intact.

When we tell our stories, and encourage others to share theirs, we are promoting positivity and optimism. Our sincere curiosity of others can give them empowerment.

Acceptance

When we share who we are through storytelling, we give ourselves the gift of acceptance. Why not pass that on? The next time someone shares a story with you, keep some things in mind. This person has chosen to share with you. Maybe they are hesitant because they think you will find it uninteresting, or you will judge them, or start to look around the room. Please remember they are sharing their story and hoping to receive the best gift there is, the gift of acceptance!

Reflection Questions

1. What kinds of stories do you like to tell? What makes them your favorites?

2. What kind of things do you think are significant in your journaling?

3. When you read stories and don't finish them, what is it that turns you off of the story?

4. If you have a favorite author or speaker, what is it that keeps you returning to their work?

Memories in Storytelling

By: Evelyn Mosley

*"Memories too often die with their owner,
and time too often surprises us by
running out."*

~William Zinsser

"Mem'ries light the corners of my mind. Misty water-colored memories of the way we were." This was one of my favorite songs in the seventies that was sung by Barbara Streisand.

Memories—The Best Toolbox!

Our memories are a wonderful toolbox from which our stories can be drawn. Our life experiences are what help us to create these memories. These experiences can be both happy and sad, but they become our memories.

As a small child growing up in Chicago, my mother's brother Uncle Forest would ask me every year what I wanted to be when I grew up. One year I said I wanted to be a nurse. That Christmas my Uncle Forest came with a wrapped gift box that was filled with a royal blue nurse cape with red on the inside, a white nurse cap, and a black nurse bag that had medical supplies like bandages and a stethoscope inside. I was so happy to receive this gift. I could mimic my aunt, Willa Mae who was an actual nurse. Occasionally my Aunt Willa Mae and Uncle Buddy would come by the house after work. My Aunt Willa Mae would be adorned in her nurse uniform which consisted of a white dress, worn with white stockings, white shoes, and a white nurse cap. She even had a royal blue cape with red on the inside liner exactly like mine and a black bag with a real stethoscope inside. How I admired her professional look. I often could be seen listening to the heart of my Barbie dolls. Sometimes I would even listen to my uncle's heart with this stethoscope. I remember having hours and hours of fun with my nurse kit. I felt so grown up and special until I got my first period and all that blood in my pajamas scared the life out of me. At that moment, my desire to become a nurse went right out the window. I no longer went around the house listening to the heart of my Barbie dolls or anyone else's heart for that matter.

My Uncle Forest, who is the third oldest of my mom's siblings was always fostering my imagination of what I wanted to be when I grew up. At the time I did not realize that he was helping me to establish my goals of what I wanted my adult future to look like. I did not have a dad in the home growing up, but I had plenty of male role models in my family.

My Uncle Forest was the dad of two boys, and he always had a Doberman pincher. My uncle raised Dobermans to be military and police protective animals, and one of his dogs was named "Micky." She was a beautiful shiny black color with a brown-patch on her breast. This dog was extremely aggressive. Anytime we came to their brownstone to visit, Micky would have to be housed in a closet to prevent her from tearing us limb from limb. Micky would let you come in, but you took a notable risk trying to leave that house. Mickey could not be trusted to sniff around you for familiarity like other dogs could because as protection dogs could not be friendly to potential threats to their handlers. Growing up, our family had a series of dogs of assorted sizes and colors, so I really was not afraid to be around them. Micky, however, was a different story. I appreciated her being behind a closed door anytime I visited.

I remember one visit my brother, sister and I were in the process of leaving our Uncle Forest's home when we heard a loud thump at the closet door, and out flew Micky. I jumped up on the piano seat and Micky quickly nipped at my winter-gloved right hand. I could feel her sharp teeth grappling at my small fingertips. Uncle Forest quickly grabbed Micky by her collar and escorted her back to the closed room. This time he locked the door behind him. He came to investigate my hand while asking if I was okay. "I think I am," I said. There was no visible damage to my finger, no blood, only my knit glove was a bit frayed. I knew my heart

13

was beating fast because I knew that a dog attack by Micky would be the end of my young life. In that moment instead of our uncle taking us back home, he gave us a big bowl of ice cream instead. For me, ice cream could solve any of life's problems. It was vanilla, though the flavor did not matter to me. I absolutely loved ice cream. Still, to this day my brother, sister and I reminisce over this story. They both were happy that their big sister took a bite for the team.

But not all memories are good memories.

The creator of the Peter Pan character, J.M. Barrie who was also a Scottish novelist and playwright once said, "God gave us memory so that we might have roses in December."

The ability to forget bad times, and remember good times is a true gift. The fact is, that even though birth and many other things in life are painful and traumatic, we have the tendency to block out these terrible events. We all have this special ability: to contemplate happy memories and happy times when we are suffering. This is what is meant by roses in December. I really like that quote by J.M. Barrie.

Evelena

I grew up as the oldest sibling, so I created my alter-ego and older sister, Evelena. I always wanted an older sister. She was just two years older than I, not old enough to be bossy over me, but to be my friend. Evelena was adventurous, she loved to go fast on her bike, and she really, really admired her red hair, which she always wore parted down the middle in two pigtails. Evelena also loved her freckles. Of course, she was my imaginary alter because everyone knows that dark-skinned black girls don't have freckles with red pigtails. You do know that, **right**? It's interesting how I created this image of Evelena because personally, I knew no other person who had those physical attributes.

One Christmas I received that gift of all the gifts that I really, truly wanted. Every Saturday for the past three years my grandmother Lena and I would walk past the downtown bike store. A beautiful brand-spanking-new Schwinn bike would be showcased in the curb view front window. I admired this bike and told my mom for three Christmases that I had to have it. The way the sunlight would hit those chrome spokes on the tire was spectacular. With my long flowing red braided pigtails, I knew I just had to have that bike. It was white with a pink accent around the frame, pink and white tassels dangling from the handlebars, silver chrome on both the front and back bumpers, silver chrome spokes on both wheels, a white wanna-be leather

15

seat, and a white basket to carry all my stuff on the front of those tassel driven handlebars. No training wheels were on this bike, though at this moment in time, I do not know how to ride a two-wheel bike. But that did not stop me from taking my bike out to the highest dirt hill on the block. Adorned with my red shirt over my head (my fake hair) and my mother's eyebrow pencil dotted all over my face for freckles, with my cousin Therial's encouragement, he and I hiked to the top of the dirt hill so I could learn how to ride my brand-spanking-new Schwinn. Therial was one of 4 boys in my aunt and uncle's house. I only asked for his help because he was my favorite cousin at the time. I did not stop to think of the consequences of him not having any sisters and how he would care for me during this learning experience.

Once we arrived at the top of that dirt hill, I was exhausted and scared. I was ready to take this adventure of riding my two-wheeled bike down this hill. I mounted that white bike seat--no helmet needed. (They were not required in the sixties.) Therial told me to hold my legs out away from the petals, which I properly did and down the hill I flew. I thought the wind was going to knock my shirt (pretend hair) and freckles right off me.

Whew, what a ride! I got up off the ground only to see Therial holding his belly with his head tilted backward while laughing loudly enough for the Heavens to hear him. My right knee was spewing blood like an erupted volcano. I had broken branches all over me with scratches as evidence all over my face, legs, and arms from running into those bushes at the bottom of that dirt hill.

Well, at least that is what I remember.

Seven Truths of Writing

When recording your stories, you need to not only dive into your memories, but you must also make them visible to your audience. Storytelling that is only in an oral form can be lost to future generations, but in written form can become a legacy. I would like to divert here to talk about storytelling in the form of writing. A written story can be made interesting by including a string of your memories inside of it. You can even write a memoir which is nothing more, but pages of sentences filled with your memories. American writer and storyteller Robin Moore once said, *"Inside each of us is a natural-born storyteller, waiting to be released."* Do you agree?

Inside my writing, you will always find a story or two gathered from my memories. Without life experiences, there would be no memory.

I opened my chapter with another favorite quote written by a celebrated American writer known for his influential contributions to nonfiction writing, William Zinsser. His quote is as follows:

"Memories too often die with their owner, and time too often surprises us by running out."

How profound is that statement? There are seven truths writers can learn from Mr. Zinsser. Let us review them.

Truth #1. Good writing is good writing. No matter the genre. If nonfiction is where you do your best writing, then write nonfiction. I prefer nonfiction because of the transparent stories that I enjoy writing about.

Truth #2. The right method is the one that works for you. There are all kinds of writers and all kinds of methods. Use whatever method that helps you to say what you want to say. That is the right method for you. For example, there are three main writing styles: descriptive, analytical, and reflective. I like to think that I am more of a reflective style writer who uses a lot of descriptions. I reach back to my memories when I write. I guess in some strange way I think my memories are interesting, thus they will make a great story.

Truth #3. You can only write for yourself. If you write for yourself, you will reach the people you want to write for. If you are writing for other people, such as for your editor you will end up not writing for anyone. When you write for yourself you will make your writing more personal and relatable. People love to read about other people's stories, how they handled a specific situation, and what the outcome of that situation was.

Truth #4. The secret to memorable writing is knowing when to end the story. When you are ready to stop, stop. "If you have presented all the facts and made the point you want to make, look for the nearest exit." I am guilty of exiting before all the facts are given. This message resonates for me every time I try to duck out of my current writings, a grief devotion. Each week has its own chapter that begins with a personal story. I do not always give the reader enough of my personal story to present a clear picture of what I want them to know.

Truth #5. Your draft will never be perfect. "Writing is like a good watch; it should run smoothly and have no extra parts." Multiple rewrites are the essence of writing well. It has never been difficult for me to rewrite because I never think what I said the first time is perfect. Now if an editor tells me to rewrite, I can get into my feelings and think, "What do you mean this was not perfectly said?" The truth of the matter is that you did not write it perfectly. Rewrites are your friend.

Truth #6. The writers who stick to their memories are inevitably the most relatable. Writers are driven by a compulsion to put some part of themselves on paper. The person on the paper is usually stiffer than the person who sat down to write. Find the real man or woman behind the tension. This is another opportunity for a rewrite.

Truth #7. The solution is elimination. The secret of explicit writing is to strip every sentence to its cleanest components.

Many of these truths and quotes come from William Zinsser's book, "Writing Well." I will expand on these truths to help see how they apply to your writing.

Good writing is good writing

I agree that a writer should write what they like, which is also what they are probably good at. I earlier stated that I prefer nonfiction however, I have been throwing my hat in the poetry arena. I started writing what I call "poetry of a life" where I write about people that I have known in my life who are no longer living in this universe. I looked up what category poetry is considered. I read that poetry is the most common nonfiction. It is said to be nonfiction because the poet's feelings and emotions are shown through their writing. That makes sense, doesn't it?

Spoken word poetry is about dramatic storytelling. Sacrificial Poets artist director Kane "Novakane" Smego started a three-day residency at UNC Charlotte. It involved teaching college students and visiting local schools to teach them about the art of busting a rhyme. He started the class with a piece about him growing up in Durham with a single mother. The poem went like this:

I swear allegiance to my X-Chromosome
The one my mother gave me
The one that pushed mops for 17 years so we
could eat
I swear allegiance to my X-Chromosome
'Cause Mama Was My Guardian
Papa Was A Rolling Stone…

I absolutely loved his storytelling about growing up. It spoke to the message he was trying to tell the audience about his upbringing. It was to the point that he came from a strong mom who he highly respected for what she brought to the table.

Now, I am not saying that my poetry writing is going to be this good, but it gives me a great reference point. I can feel Kane's heart of love through his opening words. And I wasn't there to hear it, I read it. That is what your writing should do to the reader. They should be able to feel your emotions on your page.

That is what I call "good writing."

Don't be afraid to let your emotions flow through your words. Your reader wants to feel what you feel. That is an ideal way for them to connect with you. Isn't that one of the purposes of writing is to have your reader connect with you? That's what I want as a writer. I want the reader to identify that my story could have very well been their story.

The secret is knowing when to end the story

Knowing when to end the story is the biggest concern I have as a writer. The more I reread my writing the more I change and add to my writing. Perhaps that is the art of rewriting, but at some point, that story must end.

Writer William Zinsser says, "If you have presented all the facts and made the point you want to make, look for the nearest exit." The rewrites can sometimes get you into trouble with your endings. If you are writing in a storytelling form, we know all stories have a beginning and an ending. Please keep that specific point in mind. It follows this rule very clearly.

You know how your story began, and you know how your story ends. When you reflect on my story of Evelena at the beginning of this chapter, you read that at the beginning of the story,

Evelena wanted to learn how to ride her brand-new Schwinn bike. In the end, you're left in suspense that in her first experience riding her bike, she went to the top of a hill and went down that hill—feet off the pedals, red shirt on her head, eyes wide, and screaming all the way. The story ended with Evelena being covered in branches from the bushes at the end of the hill and bloody body parts. The ending never says whether she went back out to the top of that hill and that she eventually learned how to ride that bike. At the end of the story, the writer leaves it to the reader to make their own ending. Having a **suspenseful** ending to your story only adds to your story.

Your draft will never be perfect

When you are putting that first draft to paper it will consist of your raw thoughts written as you are thinking them. It is where your emotions are completely laid out on the paper for all to read. Of course, we want to think that everything we write is written perfectly and that our logical thinking is perfect, but I can assure you that your first draft will be far from perfect. Your punctuation, misspelled words, and grammar will more than likely need some refreshing. Don't feel bad or insulted if someone points these things out to you. This is where the rewriting begins. I love to rewrite because not only are the obvious errors of grammar corrected but I also find I have left out other important facts I want the reader to know. My story may not have included some important details that I needed the reader to know so that they could fully understand my story. Your story should end when all you want to say about that story has been said. It may take you several drafts(rewrites) to get to that conclusion. Be patient and keep writing.

Stories based on memories are the most relatable

Have you ever noticed that once you begin that second rewrite or draft your posture begins to loosen up? You're not that stiff writer you were when you first sat down at your computer. Your thoughts are clearer, and you find you have many more personal words to put in your story than you originally thought. This is where you get immersed in your emotions about the story. For example, when I first started writing about Evelena, I had completely omitted all the details about her Schwinn bike, like the silver chrome on the spokes of the tire and her white basket on the handlebars that carried her Barbie dolls. Adding these small details will allow the reader to have a complete visual picture of Evelena's bike. The reader does not have to insert any of their imaginings in the storyline regarding how her bike looks. Adding those small touches like the brand name of the bike, the color of the bike, the color of the seat, etch now makes that bike relatable to the reader. Perhaps when you were growing up you had that exact bike!

The solution is elimination

When we first draft our story, we find that our story can be filled with a lot of filler words. As a writer, we must be willing to strip each sentence down to use the fewest words possible to describe fully what we want the reader to know. Your writing should be specific and detailed, which should give you the cleanest sentence for your reader's understanding. When I first drafted Evelena, I described her hair as being parted down the middle and worn as a braided ponytail. One of my nonpaid beta readers said there was no such thing as hair drawn back, braided into a ponytail that was parted down the middle. Well, I knew that was her opinion because she had not grown up in my ethnic household. Braided ponytails were a real thing for African American girls with long hair. It was a quick and easy hairstyle for our busy moms that would cause the least fuss from their daughter getting her hair combed. So, I looked up the word ponytail and it said a ponytail could be braided. It also used the word "pigtail", so I immediately changed my word from ponytail to pigtail because that word more accurately portrayed my image of Evelena. Besides that, I thought it could be possible that someone else from a different ethnic background could also get confused by my description of Evelena.

Never be afraid to dig deeper into your writing for word clarity. If you need to eliminate a word so that your writing becomes clearer to your reader, then ELIMINATE. Our goal as a writer is to write our story with so much clarity that the reader feels like they have a complete understanding. We want our writing to put the reader in our pages so that they see themselves. We want our story to become relatable.

Conclusion

Evelena is my imaginary person who I only have fond memories of. Being the oldest sibling of three, taking care of the two youngest siblings I was entrusted to care for was not always fun. Evelena helped to make my childhood fun. She was energetic, she had freckles and red hair, something I did not have, nor could I have had. She was brave and adventurous, all the things in my own identity were not. Would I change anything in my childhood? Not a single word! Evelena has been lovingly held in my memories for over six decades of my life.

I encourage you to dig into your memories. Perhaps there is a story or two that you would like to share between the pages of a book. Remember what I said earlier, people like to read about the life of others and how they handled a particular situation.

I wish you all the best in digging out your memories and turning them into a memorable story for others to read.

Reflection Questions

1. Memories are a powerful tool for drafting a book. What is your most interesting childhood memory?

2. What story in this chapter stood out the most to you and why?

3. I referenced several quotes in this chapter. Do you have a favorite quote?

4. "Inside each of us is a natural-born storyteller waiting to be released." What is your story?

5. Which of the seven writer's truths speaks to you?

What Makes a Good Story for a Speaker?

By: Randy Prier

"Make a point, tell a story"

~Bill Cove

Introduction

The late Bill Gove, Certified Speaking Professional (CSP), member of the Council of Peers Award for Excellence (CPAE) Speaker Hall of Fame, and a Toastmasters International Golden Gavel Award winner, was generally acknowledged as the Father of the Public Speaking Profession. He founded the National Speakers Association (NSA), an organization dedicated to helping professional speakers become better and build their businesses. Michael Aun, himself a professional speaker and the 1978 Toastmasters World Champion of Public Speaking, said in 2013, "Every major speaking personality I've met in the past 40 years has pointed to Bill Gove as a source of inspiration and information in their speaking career." From his many years as a salesman for the 3M company, Gove became a master storyteller. He could take a single event and weave from it a riveting story full of fascinating word pictures that delivered a powerful message. Encapsulated in the quote above was his key lesson for anyone who wanted to become an effective public speaker, i.e., the best way to illustrate the point(s) you want to leave with your audience is to tell a compelling story. In fact, during my more than 40 years in Toastmasters—a worldwide oral communication and leadership training organization— when providing training on speech preparation, I have often paraphrased Gove's advice to say that the essence of a good public speech is to "tell a story, make a point, tell another story, make another point . . .."

The purpose of this chapter is to describe some of the elements that make for good stories to use in a public speech, stories that serve to illustrate the speaker's message. But first, why do stories matter? Long before there were movies, TV, radio, books, or even written languages, humans were storytellers. Spoken around a fire at night, stories told by wise men or elders conveyed the beliefs, legends, and shared knowledge/experiences of the teller's extended family group or tribe. The stories were memorized and passed on from generation to generation, becoming the lore that held the group together. But the stories not only passed on knowledge and beliefs, they also entertained and helped group members develop empathy for the trials of life and feelings of others. They also provided models of conduct and inspired creativity.

While sitting around a fire is no longer the primary environment in which stories are shared, they remain the mainstay for providing information, entertainment, and life lessons, though now through all kinds of media. Stories capture our interest much more easily than a dry recitation of facts because they bring to life relatable experiences that illustrate the points the teller wants to share. Stories evoke empathy for the characters that populate the narratives and humanize the situations portrayed. Besides, we simply want to know how the story turns out! I hope you can see now why engaging stories are critical to public speakers.

What makes a good story for a public speaker?
Illustrating Point(s) or Ideas

First, the story obviously must clearly illustrate the points or ideas the speaker wants to convey. For example, there's the story about The Elephant Rope:

> A man was observing a group of elephants (it could have been in a zoo, a circus, or a nature preserve). He was confused by the fact that these huge creatures were being held by only a small rope tied to their front leg. No chains, no cages. It was obvious the elephants could break away from their bonds at any time, but for some reason, they did not.

31

He saw a trainer nearby and asked why these animals just stood there and made no attempt to get away. "Well," the trainer said, "when they are very young and much smaller, we use the same size rope to tie them and, at that age, it's enough to hold them, even if they try to get loose. As they grow up, they are conditioned to believe they cannot break away. They believe the rope can still hold them, so they never try to break free."

For the message, this story could be used to show how we can become conditioned to believe we can't do something. To achieve our full potential, we must understand how we've been conditioned and work hard to overcome it. These animals could at any time break free from their bonds, but because they were conditioned to believe they couldn't, they were stuck right where they were. People, on the other hand, have the possibility of breaking free from their conditioning if they put their mind to it.

But a story can be used to demonstrate more than one point. For example, like the elephants, how many of us go through life hanging onto a belief that we cannot do something, simply because we failed at it once before? The message: Failure is part of learning; we never truly fail until we stop trying. So, we should never give up the struggle in life.

The elephant story is an old one that's in the public domain. It's quite acceptable to use such third-party sources if you're not able to come up with a personal story that fits your point. But often the best stories are ones from your personal experience. They are the most authentic and enable you to really get into the retelling. I will use such a story later.

Four Key Elements

Beyond making the point and being personal, if possible, there are four other key elements that are important in a good story for a speaker.

- First, a good story should appeal to the hearer's intellect, i.e., it should make the audience think. Have I ever been in a situation like that? If not, how should I prepare or react? What impact should this chain of events make on how I will deal with similar situations in the future?

- Next, a story should be relatable and appeal to the listeners' emotions. Did it make your listeners happy or sad, angry or depressed? Were they able to empathize with how the characters must have felt in the circumstances they experienced?

- Third, if you can inject some humor into the story, it can make you more likable and therefore make your message more acceptable to your audience. Did they laugh or at least smile?

- Finally, a story should touch on important issues in the human experience. Did the story give some different ways of looking at things or provide useful life lessons?

Let's look at a personal story of mine and test it for the inclusion of these elements:

As I have mentioned I have long been a member of Toastmasters International. I frequently compete in the organization's speech contests, my favorite being the Humorous contest. (Other types of Toastmasters speech contests are the International, Tall Tales, Evaluation, and Table Topics.) Each time I compete, my goal is to win at the highest local level, the district, and I have done so five times in four different types of contests. However, in the late 1990's and early 2000's, the best I could do in the Humorous contest was second place. So, out of frustration, I put together a speech titled "The Second Place Curse."

The burden of the speech is that, in contests, if you always place third or lower, you probably aren't meant to win and should give up. However, if you consistently hear the words, "The second-place winner is ___(You),'' you get a case of the "if only's." Holding thumb and index finger about a half inch apart, you tell yourself, "I was this close. If only I had taken this bit out and put another bit in. Or if only I had better judges, or a better speaking position," and so forth. Therefore, because you came so close over and over you feel compelled to keep on trying, only to fail again. You are a victim of the "second-place curse." It was not fate, destiny, or lack of ability, it was a case of bad luck.

One year, reaching the district finals with the "Curse" speech, I had an early speaking position, and the speech received raucous laughter. I felt good about my chances. Then came a young fellow who delivered a great speech-lots of laughs. You guessed it, "The second-place winner is Randy Prier." I put on a brave face as I accepted my second-place trophy, but I was more depressed than I had ever been in Toastmasters. I second-guessed everything, finally realizing that by talking about second place I was actually giving the judges permission to put me second—a bitter lesson. But I got over it, kept trying, and finally in 2010, I won, and again in 2015.

So, did this story appeal to the intellect? Would a listener perhaps question my decision to craft a speech almost destined to render the outcome I was complaining about? Would they understand that failure is only failure if you give up trying?

Certainly, the story had the potential to evoke strong emotions. Is there anyone who hasn't experienced failure trying to achieve something they desperately wanted? Could they not relate to the depression or at least the sadness I felt?

Was there humor in the story? What about the whole concept of the second-place curse and the "if only's?"

Finally, did the story touch upon important themes? How many people fail to find success and give up? Is it not vital to teach the importance of persistence and not giving up?

Conclusion

Throughout human history, stories have been the way to communicate information, entertain, and promote common understanding among all peoples. They are an especially engaging way for a speaker to make his points. This has not changed with the development of modern technology. Yet the special resonance, the human touch, of people speaking in person before groups has not diminished.

Our history is full of outstanding speakers who inspired and entertained audiences with stories full of humor and profound life lessons. Mark Twain was a renowned novelist, but he also traveled the lecture tour in the latter half of the 19th century, giving his audiences rollicking stories full of simple wisdom, based on his adventures on the Mississippi River and out West. Later came Will Rogers, the "Cowboy Philosopher" who intertwined commentary on current issues with homespun stories about his life as a cowboy and rope trick entertainer in Wild West shows. He too never missed a chance to comment on the foibles of politicians of the day. More recently, Oprah Winfrey, a wildly successful television personality and businesswoman, regularly talks about her own rags-to-riches story. Billionaire Richard Branson talks about his many failures and how he persisted to come back and succeed. Comedians Ellen DeGeneres and Jim Gaffigan exaggerate for the sake of humor, but the stories in their routines obviously come from their own lives.

The stories these speakers and so many others share appeal to minds, rouse emotions, evoke laughter, and cause us to confront important ideas in a way that cold, electronic communication can't. You can be an influential speaker by sharing your lessons in stories. Those stories and the lessons they convey tend to be remembered long after listeners hear them and can leave a lasting impression. So, if you dream of becoming a popular and successful public speaker, build a portfolio full of entertaining and powerfully meaningful stories.

<u>Reflection Questions</u>

1. What are your thoughts about the key elements to a good story? Should a story appeal to the intellect, the emotions, the sense of humor, and to a sense of importance? What elements would you add or take away?

2. Try to come up with a story that might be used to illustrate a point(s) in a speech.

   - Start by thinking about some incident that has happened to you, your work colleagues, your family, or your friends in the last few days or weeks (you can go back further if necessary). Try to think about something that involved a silly mistake or accident or an everyday occurrence that had an unexpected turn of events. Or perhaps it was something more impactful that could illustrate a life lesson, either small or large.

- Jot down who was involved and briefly describe what happened.

- Now think about what events in the story might make someone think about what happened and how it impacted you or others.

- What emotions were evoked?

- Was there something humorous about what happened?

- Finally, think about the importance of this event to you or others.

3. Now that you've gone through this process, see if can apply it to other events that happened as you were growing up, during your school days, in your relationships with friends and romantic interests, work/career experiences, and so on. As you repeat this process you can build up a catalogue of stories that could be used in future speeches.

Crafting Characters for Your Stories

By Rebecca Fegan

"When writing a novel, a writer should create living people; people not characters. A character is a caricature."

~ Ernest Hemmingway

The Nature of Characters

Every story will have characters. They might not all be human; they may not even be animate! The characters will carry the burden of the message you want to give the readers. Is it a tale that teaches a moral? Does it have a point to make? Does it teach an aspect of life most would miss? How do you design the characters in your story?

Just open that can of worms! Hemingway, in this quote, was discussing characters in a novel, but even when telling a short story, you are creating a **reality** for your readers. It is a chance to put themselves into a place of your design as observers. But they won't understand it or inhabit that world for long if the players are mannequins.

When telling stories, you can start with people you know as the characters. You may already know what they look like, what they do for a living, and why they are in that particular place at that particular time. But there might be several people present in the scene, and if you have time constraints or length constraints, you don't have the luxury of introducing all the faces in the crowd to get across your point.

Instead of introducing us to all the participants, you can choose one person, then you combine the qualities of the rest of the people into that one character. This makes the message clearer, and it even makes the character more distinct. This is a new being of your own creation, even if it is based on several people you know.

For instance, in the movie, "The Patriot" the protagonist is an amalgamation of several real people. Rodat, the writer of the screenplay, has said that Martin, the main character, is a composite character based on four historical men:

- Andrew Pickens
- Francis Marion
- Daniel Morgan
- and Thomas Sumter.

The story would have been closer to the factual circumstances if it had included all of these characters, but the movie would have been six hours long!

Major and minor characters require attention to detail. You want to make them believable, complex, and autonomous. Your characters are reflections of your mental, physical, and spiritual selves—different aspects, good and bad. These are explorations into human thought, emotion, and behavior.

Character Sheets

One thing you can do is build a Character Sheet. You have several categories to fill in.

- physical features
- strengths/weaknesses
- work
- family
- back story—age, culture, location…
- hobbies, skills

You may already know that this character is tall and well-built. Then the fun comes in. Here are some examples of how to build a character.

1. **You can use dice to choose the aspects of this character!** Roll a 4-sided die for hair color. Roll a different die for accent, and another for strengths (unless you know what strengths this character needs in the story already). This bit of randomness can give you a picture in your own mind that will help you recall all the aspects you've designed.

2. **You can base the character on someone you have in mind.** You know James is a big teddy bear, but he's very intimidating. He works at a warehouse. You suspect he sneaks out at night and dons a cape and a mask... So, you imbue him with special powers. You can hear his voice in your head when you write the dialog. You understand his sense of humor. You know his dark past. You put all these characteristics on his character sheet.

3. **Put the character into the situation you've designed.** Now you have to decide how he/she will act under pressure. What do they want? How far would they go to get it? What would it take to stop them? Does that sound

like action/adventure? It also describes a morality play, a poem, a romantic comedy, or a tragedy.

Let your imagination carry you through this process.

In some video games, you choose your avatar, and you design the look and build of this character. You create the clothes they wear, the skills they have, the weapons they carry. But in a game, you cannot insert a back story and you cannot describe their moral code except in the choices you make as your avatar transverses this world he or she inhabits. In a story, however, you <u>do</u> have this control and it is to the benefit of your listeners and readers that you make your characters as detailed as you can.

In Ryan Avery's speech at the 2012 Toastmasters International World Championship of Public Speaking contest, "Trust is a Must," he told three stories about the quality of trust. He put himself as the main character. Well, that was easy, his character sheet probably read:

Character 1—Me.

- **Goal:** What does he want? A good relationship with the woman he's marrying.

- **Conflict:** How far would he go to get it? He determines that trust is the most important quality he should have. He reviews all the experiences when he wasn't trustworthy, the times when someone else betrayed his trust, and the price he paid.

- **Effort:** What would it take to stop him from being trustworthy? He decides that being untrustworthy only happens when he puts his desires above those of his bride-to-be. He is determined not to do that.

He tells three stories regarding trust, and each is only one minute long. He is the main character in each of those. Yet, every one of them has the elements of his character throughout.

The other characters in his stories include his mama, the sheriff, the businessman, and his future bride. Since this was a live performance, he acted out the characters, changing their tone of voice, their stance, and their accents. He gave just enough description of these minor characters to activate the audience's recognition of the stereotypes. He didn't get into detail in the description of his wife except that she was the love of his life.

Now some people not only write down the descriptions of their characters, but they also draw pictures or download characters from movies or television shows.

Here's the thing though: You do not have to give all the details of your character to your audience. Most of the time, their actions, and the reactions of the people around them in the story will give the audience a sense of this character. Look at this example:

> There was Jack, sitting at the workbench but instead of designing the bomb, he was crocheting. Ann was surprised. "Is that really Jack? Jack, the guy who carries the jeep across the river; Jack the guy that takes down twenty-one terrorists with his bare hands; Jack who plays flamenco guitar?"

Do you see how her reaction gives you a whimsical view of the main character, Jack? It makes it appear that crocheting is somewhat out of character for him. This might have been a roll-of-the-die choice on his character sheet, or you may have been up all night watching Laural and Hardy movies. It serves to give your character, Jack, a more human quality.

The nice thing with character sheets is that they give you the flexibility to make changes as the character grows throughout the story...new skills, new awareness, new values, new relationships.

The Purpose of the Character

The story is built around the character, or the character is built around the plot.

Let's say you want to write a story about an alien who visits a sleepy little town in Nebraska. Who is the main character? It depends on the message you want to get across, doesn't it? Is the alien what you want to concentrate on, or is it the people it encounters? Is there a moral to the story? What would be the point of the story?

- Not every alien is trying to take over the world.
- What would you do if you landed on an alien planet? What would they assume about you?
- Just because they have better technology doesn't mean they're more ethically evolved.
- Before you hit an alien with a stick, you should probably discover whether they explode when you hit them with a stick. Start with a small rock...

The other thing you need to remember is that in a complete character, they will <u>not</u> be harmonious. Be truthful. Don't you ever argue with yourself? "Should I tell him he's got mustard on his tie? What concern is it to me? Would I want to be told I have mustard on my tie? Will I be wondering about this in two hours?" Doesn't everyone have those moments of doubt after they make a decision? That's why they have special training for salespeople on what to do to avoid buyer's remorse. There are shelves of books that deal with impostor syndrome, indecisiveness, and procrastination. Your characters cannot be perfect, or they become less believable.

When you put your character into the action of the story, if he doesn't make mistakes, he becomes super-human. How does he handle the internal conflicts in addition to the conflicts he faces in the plot?

Imagine the teacher who goes into the rowdy room and says, "Everyone sit down and open your books to page 85." He does not repeat himself, and he does not raise his voice. The students comply—without complaint, and without noise! Does that make you wonder how he has this power over his students? What is he thinking that allows him to know what to say and do to get their attention? How has he established this rapport? He is instantly complex, and now you have built up some curiosity. We're curious about his students, his classroom, his background, the school, and the subject matter. Why? Because his simple communication and the direction given to the students were instantaneously acted upon. This is out of character for most circumstances you can imagine.

You, however, have the character sheet. You know that he has charisma and a wicked left hook, and your audience doesn't know that yet. They don't know he's been in the school system for four years and took on a gang leader in the parking lot, putting him in the hospital for a week with a broken cheekbone. You work that into the story, but you also include that he visited the gang leader in the hospital and helped him learn to do math.

Then there are other aspects you introduce bit by bit that fill out the character. You don't give the whole description of the character in one or two pages of your story (or one to two minutes in your speech), but add snippets throughout the story.

But it all starts with the character page.

Here's an example of a more comprehensive character page. Remember that you will not be exposing all the aspects of the character to your audience—just enough to give them a general idea of who this person is. The columns are just wide enough to put check marks by them.

Character Sheet   Name:

Physical aspects

Gender	
Height	
Weight	
Build	
Hair color	
Eye color	
Handedness	
Dexterity	
Quickness	
Speed	
Coordination	
Voice range	
Voice projection	

Mental aspects	
Intelligence	
Intuition	
Demeanor	
Memory	
Problem-solving	
Deductive reasoning	
Inductive reasoning	
Strategic thinking	
Tactical thinking	
Language Command	

Mental aspects cont.

Numbers Command	
Science	
Arts	
Engineering	
Pattern Recognition	

Emotional aspects	
Empathetic	
Solitary	
Gregarious	
Extroverted	
Introverted	
Confident	
Loyal	
Trustworthy	
Reverent	
Respectful	
Persistent	
Kind	
Observant	
Present	
Pessimistic	
Optimistic	
Creative	
Unimaginative	

You can use the back of the page as space for descriptions:

- How they walk
- what kind of accent they have
- anomalies that you think are important to note
- and maybe cultural or family backgrounds and traditions.

You can get into details like in Ryan's speech where his phrase throughout was "Trust is a Must." Remember that in Forrest Gump, his go-to was "Stupid is as stupid does?" And who can forget, "I'll be back?" in the Schwarzenegger movies?

Problem-solving, the story behind the story
For the main characters, you need to have a back story. I do this on the back of my character sheets.

I. Where did this character grow up?
   A. Rural? Small town? City?
   B. What country? And where in that country?
II. What was his/her home life like?
   A. Big family? Small family? Blended? 1 or 2 parents? Intergenerational?
   B. What did his/her parents do for a living?
   C. Any trauma?

III. What kinds of relationships is your character involved in? Friends? Significant Others? Pets? Rivals?

IV. How does this character come to be in the situation you put him/her in?

    A. How does this character get to the location where the action takes place?

    B. Does he/she work with a team or solo?

    C. How does he/she come across the antagonist/protagonist/minor characters?

    D. Why does he/she get involved?

V. What is your character's go-to first reaction to conflict? Action or communication?

"Clark stood looking up at the skyscrapers and wondered to himself, 'How did a kid from Hendley, Nebraska, population 20, find himself as a journalist in a well-respected paper in the biggest city in the state? If only his parents (the manager of the feed store and the elementary school teacher) could see him now!'" This is cheesy, but you see how not all the information is delivered at once. In addition, much of the plumbing you did into this character will never be revealed to the audience.

(Now Obviously, this is not the Clark Kent you see in the movies or the graphic novels. This is the real guy they based the stories on, and they just changed the locations to protect his identity…just like adding glasses protected Clark Kent in the movies and novels.)

"As Clark untangled the cars of the wrecked train, he remembered when he had picked up and thrown the tractor that had pinned his father when it overturned and the look on his father's face. He was just thirteen at the time." Now you know he has a history of moving very large objects with relative ease.

When you finish this character-building exercise, you know where he shops, what he drives, where he has lunch, who he goes to for advice, who his friends are, and his set of values. If you met him, you'd recognize him. You know the clothes he wears, his favorite activities, and his least favorites.

There is one scene in one of a myriad of Superman shows on TV, where Superman is talking to his teenage sons, and one of them says, "I've MET Superman!" Then Clark removes his glasses. Wait, you mean that in all of the 17 years this kid has been alive, this was the first time he had seen his father without his glasses? It was supposed to be a dramatic reveal. Clark then picks up the farm truck, holds it over his head, and then rises into the air with it. So obviously removing his glasses was not the most convincing clue to his real identity. If the kid had been a smart aleck, he might have said, "You mean that all this time we've been riding the bus when Mom said you needed the truck to get to work?!"

This indicates that the character sheet for Clark's sons was incomplete, unless, under the mental acuity category the sheet described them as "not very bright."

As you read through the *Lord of the Rings* by Tolkien, you discover that Pippin and Merry have amazing survival skills because Tolkien reveals their special talents a bit at a time. The first time you hear Pippin sing, however, it's a revelation.

Some of the most climactic moments in stories, films, and speeches come from the unexpected discoveries about the characters. And these are borne of your imagination and personal knowledge that you put into your character sheets.

The point is that the characters you create must have a purpose in solving a problem. You have to imbue them with the characteristics they will need to have to do this. Sometimes the characters do not have everything they need, and part of your plot will reveal how they come to learn the skills, gain the insight, the intuition, the experience, and even the physical tools they will need for the climax of the story.

Introductions, Please

Now that you have characters, you have to introduce them in the story. You understand that stories are just a timeline that you share with your audience. It's a specific place in a specific moment under specific circumstances.

Imagine you're looking through a telescope at a rather barren part of the sky and you see a streak. How did you come to look at that particular part of the sky when the streak appeared? What if you had looked at that same spot a day before or a day after? What if you had been seeking for a streak like that—would you have aimed the telescope at this position in the sky? This is the perspective you give to your audiences. It is a piece of a timeline you share with them.

Each character must have a reason to inhabit this piece of the timeline.

"There they sat in the back of the van, masks on, and weapons at the ready. The five of them only knew the code names of their compatriots and the plan, and they had never seen each other's faces."

Dropping these characters into that timeline with no descriptions, no backstory, and no indication of why they're there, you <u>still</u> get a sense of anticipation that makes us want to know who these guys are and what they're up to. Do you have character sheets for each of them? You bet!

Introducing them to the story is a really fun, creative process. Take, for instance, crime procedurals. How many ways can you introduce the body to the audience? In the murder mysteries by Kathy Reichs, you know the introduction of the crime scene has to be particularly gross with as much gore as possible. Why? Because it's like her stories: you have to scrape away the grime and the goo to get to the bones or the substance of the mystery. A great deal of time in these books is devoted to the stories the victims tell from the autopsy table by way of the heroine's inspection of the bones.

In other procedurals, the introduction of the crime is a glimpse of the commission of the crime but with important details left out. My favorites are those, like Columbo, where the criminal's identity is only known by the audience, and it becomes a cat-and-mouse game to see if the hero can outsmart the villain.

You get an introduction to the character and some of his/her traits by way of plot. The part you must focus on is this question:

What, in this character's composition, causes them to be at that place at that time under those circumstances? In other words, why did that streak show up in the telescope? And why is it significant enough that others should see it?

Another thing to consider is the size of the hero's and villain's group: Is it one person or a small crew? Do they lead armies or tell little brothers what to do? If it is a group, how do they come into the situation?

- Do you introduce them all together like the Family Robinson or the Brady Bunch?
- Are they recruited like the Mission Impossible group?
- Did they apply for the position like the secretary at a large corporation, or did they volunteer like someone who wants to support a Habitat for Humanity project?
- Were they rescued or kidnapped so they weren't in the group voluntarily?
- Were they constructed like androids?

Consider all these different scenarios. Whatever way you choose to introduce these characters to your audience, you have to design them so they belong there and have a purpose that advances the story.

Hearing their voices

There are some circumstances when dialog will be the main tool you use to advance the plot, give a description, introduce new characters, etc.

What do you do first? Oh, go to the character sheet... of course. If you hear their voices, you can design the dialog to sound like they came organically from the character.

I think if you had a drill sergeant speaking, you wouldn't want it to sound like some erudite academic. Vulgar and coarse language would not be appropriate for the church organist. That's why you have the character sheets. You might have to misspell words to get the pronunciation of some of the slang terms or the regional dialects you might hear from your characters.

The real trick is to make sure all the characters do not sound like YOU. That has been the biggest challenge I have when I write. If you ever watch someone give a speech that has dialog in it, you understand what I mean.

The speaker changes his stance, his posture, his orientation (facing stage left instead of stage right), the tone of his voice, the pitch, and the accent in the blink of an eye so you know exactly who is speaking. He may even change his hand gestures or the pace of his words. When telling a story with dialog, you must make these changes instantaneously obvious. They may share a sense of humor, a similar background, similar experiences, but their perceptions will be different. They will express distinct emotions, contrasting opinions, and other distinguishing features that make them unique individuals.

Use your character sheet to help. Listen to people from the region you want your player to be from. Listen to people in the same age range or in the same role. Listen to how people react under stress, in joy, in sadness, and other emotions so you can describe their voices. Pay attention to the people around you, the ones on TV, or actors in movies. Practice describing how they're speaking. Are they talking fast, slow, loud, or soft? How can you tell how emotional they are? How big is the vocabulary?

I once tutored a student from Trinidad. When he spoke, I had to listen very closely because he spoke with a Caribbean accent, very fast, and slang with which I was unfamiliar. In addition, he had a stuttering problem. Learning to listen for regional dialects, slang, and voice tone is something you need to practice to get it right.

Why do you use dialog?

What the characters say is more than enough to give the setting.

Example #1: *It was a dark and stormy night...* is the beginning of Snoopy's ongoing novel, not the beginning of a good story.

Bridgit said, "I don't think I'll ever be warm again. I'm soaked to the bone!" Do you get the impression of the weather? Do you need more details? Add them into the conversation or use a description of the character's actions to give more depth.

Dialog can also be used to establish the relationship between characters. Here you have 3 characters in the room, but in the first description, you only see two of them.

Example #2: *Jeff watched her come in. She was tall, leggy, and walked slowly and deliberately to his table.* Eh. There is no involvement or emotional reaction to her entrance.

Making use of the dialog, you get this:

Greg watched Jeff as the woman entered and said, "I know you're thinking about the lyrics to *Wild Thing*... Boy, she's way out of your league. In addition, she's blonde and you like brunettes. And if you dance together, you'll have to stand on a box."

Now you have the relationship between Greg and Jeff, and Greg's observations of Jeff's reaction to the woman.

You can also use dialog to move the plot along.

Example #3: *She didn't know the neighborhood or anyone in it. Hoping she wouldn't stand out like a sore thumb; she tried mimicking the accent and learning the local customs.* Part of the charm of the story might be in her attempts to fit in.

Annabelle was about to meet her new neighbors. "Holla! Como est Yoosted?" she said, murdering the language although with the best intentions.

Maria smiled and replied, "I actually do speak English, this being New York and all."

"Rilly? Ah didn't mean any offense."

"None taken. So, what part of Florida are you from?"

"Wha, Tampa! What part of Mexico are you from?"

"Puerto Rico…"

"Is that North or South Mexico?"

Maria decided the first house-warming present she'd bring would be a map.

We've established the relationship between Maria and Annabelle, their emotional reactions to each other, and their geographical educations as well.

Next, you drop into the conflict of the story. What better way to indicate the level of conflict than using dialog?

Example #4:

- "What are you doing?" he said mildly annoyed.
- "What are you doing?" she whispered anxiously.
- "What the heck are you doing?!" he screamed, red-faced.
- "Whatcha doin' mithter?" lisped the sweet child with her teddy bear.

How do these sentences change the situation and alert the reader to the level of danger and the nature of the conflict? In what way do these examples heighten the emotional level of the audience? Dialog, then, can be a very useful tool!

How do you know if you should use dialog, then? If you've spent two minutes describing every detail of the living room, maybe it could have been done in dialog and might have been more interesting. But if your dialog consists of a philosophical discussion that does not set the scene, does not develop the plot, and worst of all, does not entertain and causes your audience to wonder if there's a test later, you can probably just use your narrator. In this case, the dialog serves only as a distraction.

Remember that all of your dialog revolves around that character sheet.

Accidental Character Crafting

You all know that crafting character sheets right from the beginning might not be the preferred way to write for many people! It may not even cross their minds! They write the story and present it. They get their book self-published or they use the story as part of a speech or presentation. What's so hard about that? Why would anyone want to go through all that trouble? This is what happens to me:

- I write the story or think of the story and blurt it out and naturally, the person I'm talking about in the story is actually **in the room**. (Gasp!) Then they say, "Hmmm, I don't remember it that way."
- I write the story generically, and someone in the audience says, "I know that guy!" when of course he doesn't as I made him up.
- I write a story and someone says, "If he truly was an accountant who spent sixteen hours at his job, how was

he able to run the twelve blocks to the train station without having a heart attack?"

- Or the audience punches holes in my story because it doesn't make sense with the characters I've chosen to present.

In a short speech, I might write my story and have a blank piece of paper near with the names of all the people. As I write, I ask myself, how is this character able to do this? Why did he do this instead of that? Would this character have said this line? Is there enough description so the audience can "see" him? Then I write it down so I won't forget.

THERE IS A SHORTCUT!!

Craft your stories about people you already know well. Then just change their names to protect the innocent.

Conclusion

You can have the greatest message, the perfect scene, and well-defined conflict, but if your characters do not hit that emotional button, your story won't have the impact. The characters need to be three-dimensional, realistic, and familiar to the audience as soon as possible, so they can cheer the hero and boo the villain and know which one is which!

I did see one movie where you were cheering for the hero and then discovered that the villain we'd identified was actually the good guy! It was a great plot twist. But it was only good because of the way the characters were established. Your characters will drive the plot and make all the action believable. In fact, they might even influence the scene where you set your story.

If you set your characters well, you could return to them over and over. This is great if you're writing sequels or establishing them as archetypes for other stories. Concentrate on your characters and let them come to life in your stories.

Reflection Questions

1. Think of your favorite character from a book or movie. What brings a smile to your face when you think of this character?

2. If you were to put this character into a character sheet, how would you describe him/her/it?

3. What characteristics would you consider heroic?

4. How do you go about imagining the emotional state of your audience when crafting a story? How do you push that emotional button?

5. When you tell a story, how does your audience react?

6. If you write or tell a humorous story, does your audience laugh because your protagonist acts counter to what is expected or acts exactly as expected?

Setting: The Other Character

By: Mark Fegan

"It was a dark and stormy night"
~ *Edward Bulwer-Lytton*
"All the world's a stage, And all the men and women merely players"
~ *William Shakespeare*

We have discussed several of the elements that go toward making a good story: characters, plot, and action to mention a few. But where does the story take place? And how do we describe that time and location without getting in the way of the story?

What is the setting?

When you are crafting a story, one of the elements you need to identify is the setting. In fact, the setting may be the most critical element to consider as you begin writing the story.

Every story takes place in a specific *location*; that location is defined by both the *time* and *place* where the action of the story occurs. The location of the story is also called the setting for the story; for this chapter, I will refer to the setting rather than the location as many people don't think about *when* as part of the location. To understand the importance of including *when* in the setting, consider a story set in New York City. Although much of the plot of the story would be the same in 1945 as in 2025, many of the details that contribute to the story will have changed between 1945 and 2025.

The setting may be a real place, or it may exist only in the mind of the storyteller. Because it plays an integral part in relating the events in the story, the setting may be considered to be another character contributing to the overall story. The setting will provide the context; in a sense, the setting provides a stage on which the other characters act out the story.

Consider this. Suppose you decide to create a story about life on the moon. What effect will that setting, the moon, have on how the characters in the story react? What complications will the characters face because they are living on the moon? How will the moon's gravity, approximately 16% of the earth's gravity, have on how they act? If they decide to return to Earth, how will the higher gravity impact their actions? One impact of the moon's smaller size and lower gravity is the lack of a life-sustaining atmosphere on the moon's surface. How does the lack of an atmosphere impact your characters? How does it impact the way they live and work? What additional complications and/or problems do the characters face because the story is about life on the moon?

As you plan and write your story, you need to be aware of the setting and you need to communicate that setting in a way that enhances the impact of the story. The setting needed for the story should not interfere with the narrative of the story. To accomplish that goal will likely take some planning. You might even consider the setting to be that extra, albeit hidden, character. As Rebecca Fegan suggested in her chapter *Crafting Characters for Your Stories*, you may even consider creating a character sheet for the story's setting.

One additional comment about your story's setting. How the setting is presented is somewhat dictated by the medium used to tell the story. If you are writing the story intending to present it in a written form, you will need to describe the setting. You need to be careful, however, as describing the setting for the story must not obscure the actual story!

What follows are some commonly used approaches to including the setting in the story.

Make the Story Contemporary

Making the story contemporary is a technique that allows the reader, or listener, to fill in the setting based on his or her background. Basically, the author, through a narrator, provides a minimal description of the setting, both in time and place, by identifying objects the characters use and places the characters visit. The reader is expected to understand and identify both the time and place where the action occurs. Although this relieves the author of the work creating and communicating the setting, it tends to date the story. A reader/listener may need to do some outside research to help understand some of the plot points.

A good example of this technique is the Sherlock Holmes stories written by Sir Arthur Conan Doyle. The Sherlock Holmes stories were written between 1887 and 1927. Conan Doyle set the stories in late Victorian and Edwardian England. Most of the stories were set in London. Conan Doyle generally assumed that his readers would know the meaning of his references to contemporary culture. Reading the stories a century later, later, we are likely to become confused by his references to

- Hansom Cabs (a two-wheeled horse-drawn cab with a partially enclosed passenger cabin where the "driver" was seated above, behind, and outside the cabin)

- Broughams (a four-wheeled carriage with an enclosed passenger cabin where the driver was seated in front also outside the cabin)

- Crops (which refers to riding or driving crops to guide or whip a horse).

Conan Doyle compensated by concentrating most of his effort on the characters, Sherlock Holmes and John Watson.

The Narrator Simply describes the Action

In the chapter *Point of View*, Keith Jones describes the various voices that can be used when writing a story. One of those voices is in the *Third Person* in which the narrator simply describes what is happening in the story including the setting. The narrator does not interact with the characters; the narrator simply describes what is happening. In effect, the third-person narrator fills a role similar to an electronic recording device. A third-person narrator does have one advantage, however. A narrator is not bound to any one character or location. As long as the narrator simply describes what is happening, the action described may be occurring at multiple locations. (The narration should clearly identify the actual location, of course.)

The All-Seeing Narrator

In Erle Stanley Gardner's Perry Mason stories and novels, the hero of the stories is Perry Mason with the able assistance of Della Street. Most of the action centers on Perry Mason, of course, but Gardner used third-person narration to set the scene and describe the action. The characters provided the dialog that completed the action.

When the author allows the narrator the freedom to describe the action from multiple settings while hiding some of the action and the related storylines from some of the characters, as was the case in Gardner's *Case of the Shoplifter's Shoe*, (published 1938), it provides a much richer story. In this particular example, Gardner needed to describe action outside the presence of the main characters (Mason, Street, and Drake). One chapter is devoted to a scene where the District Attorney is prepping one of the prosecution witnesses; this action takes place at the District Attorney's office. Because Gardner was using a third-person narrator, the story continued without a hitch. By keeping the narrator as an uninvolved observer, Gardner was able to shift smoothly between scenes in various locations involving various characters without adversely impacting the overall flow of the story. The result is an improved experience for the reader

Although this technique may be used in written stories, you are probably more familiar with its use in visual storytelling in television shows, movies, and live dramatic productions. In visual storytelling, the setting for the story is provided by the set containing the action. The players contribute to the telling of the story through their spoken words and their actions.

In the chapter *Point of View*, Keith Jones describes the various voices that can be used when writing a story. One of those voices is the *Third Person*. Telling the story in the third person, the narrator usually describes the setting and action as it occurs. In the case of the All-Seeing narrator, there is an interesting twist that an author may choose to employ: the narrator is free to roam in time and space; the narrator can describe the action that is occurring outside the presence of the main characters. In fact, the action being described may occur with no one present to experience that action. The all-seeing narrator is not bound to any of the characters in the story!

In Andy Weir's *The Martian*, © 2011 by the Author, there is a dramatic moment when a shipment of provisions is being shipped from the Earth to Mars. The narrator describes the fatal flight of the supply rocket as the payload shifts and causes the rocket to explode. The narrator is not bound to any one physical location and describes the action *where no man has gone* before. This is an example of an all-seeing narrator

The All-Seeing Narrator on Stage

Consider the plays of the Bard, William Shakespeare.

Shakespeare set his plays in various locations in Europe and at various times. For example, *Julias Caesar* was set in and around Rome in the late first century BC. If you take time to read the play, you will find very sketchy notes about the actual setting.

As an example, for Act 1, Scene 1, the setting simply identifies the characters in the scene. There is no mention of the time or location of the action. The reader is expected to understand that the action takes place in Rome (Italy) in the spring and summer of 44 BC. Please note that the audience consisted of Londoners living in the sixteenth and early seventeenth centuries.

Also, recall that Julias Ceasar is a dramatic play. It was first performed at the Globe Theatre in London around 1599 AD. The Globe was rather primitive by today's standards; the bulk of the action in the play was presented on a nearly bare stage. There are some clues to the setting in the text of the play that are revealed as the players deliver their lines, but generally, the audience was left to fill in the setting based on their own imaginations.

You may have seen one of the movie versions of Julias Ceasar. In that case, most of the setting was provided by the production company's interpretation of Rome and the Roman Empire in 44 BC. But, if you read the actual play, you will realize what you are seeing is the director's interpretation of the actual setting.

Have a Character Describe the Action

As Keith Jones described in his chapter *Point of View*, first-person narration is provided by one of the characters in the story. That character takes an active role in the story, interacting with other characters, but, as the narrator, is responsible for providing the setting for the action as well as describing that action. Note that the first-person narrators can only describe places and actions that they can see; anything outside the presence of the narrator must be introduced via conversation with other characters.

I've already mentioned Author Conon Doyle's use of contemporary England, especially London, as part of the setting for his Sherlock Holmes stories. Conon Doyle's stories were contemporary to the time in which he wrote and published the stories. But time is only one aspect of a story's setting. The other aspect is the physical location of the action described in the story.

In most of his Sherlock Holmes stories, Conon Doyle used one of his characters, Dr. John Watson, as his narrator. Conon Doyle has Dr. Watson provided descriptions of where the action was taking place. (Admittedly, he frequently mentioned place places and expected his readers would fill in the details.) In addition to describing the location, Conon Doyle frequently uses Dr. Watson to describe the action occurring in the story. Finally, since Dr. Watson is usually one of the characters in the story, he interacts with the other characters but, as described above, he can only describe what he can see.

A good example of how Conon Doyle uses a first-person narrator is his novel *The Hound of the Baskervilles*. Originally published in 1902, the novel was written after Conon Doyle attempted to kill off Sherlock Holmes in 1893. The reading public and Conon Doyle's publisher demanded more stories of the great detective. *The Hound of the Baskervilles* was Conon Doyle's response.

In this novel, Sherlock Holmes is hired to protect Sir Henry Baskerville and solve the mystery surrounding the Baskerville family. Sherlock Holmes claims to have pressing business that requires his presence in London. As a result, Dr. Watson is sent to the Baskerville Hall located on the Dartmoor. For much of the first half of the novel, Dr. Watson attempts to investigate the mystery surrounding the Baskerville family. Because he is the narrator, he can only report events he witnesses and describe events that other characters relate to him. He can report conversations where he is present; these conversations include words he speaks.

Without giving away too much of the plot, there is a mysterious stranger on the moor, Dr. Watson and some other characters do see this person, but his identity and actions remain a mystery until Dr. Watson tracks him down. This is a critical characteristic of first-person narration; the narrator can only report what they see or what other characters relate in conversations.

Another author who uses first-person narration is Rex Stout in his Nero Wolfe stories and novels. Although centered around Nero Wolfe, the stories are narrated by Wolfe's assistant Archie Goodwin. Goodwin provides the setting, depression to World War II era New York, but generally allows the reader to fill in the details. Goodwin provides the narration to enhance the setting and describes the action. He not only engages other characters in conversation but takes part in the action, yet he can only relate what he sees and experiences.

Final Thoughts

In my chapter *Finding Your Stories,* I discussed writing stories that can be used to add depth to presentations. Although the emphasis of that chapter was on oral presentations, the elements used to create a story include when and where the action in the story takes place. That is, the setting of the story is an integral element of the story, but not usually the most important element. In other words, the setting of the story is essentially the stage upon which the story is performed. It must support the action in the story but overwhelm that action.

As an example, movies based on Shakespeare's *Romeo and Juliet* have been set in 16th century Verona, Italy (the 1968 Franco Zeffirelli film) and contemporary United States (the 1996 Baz Luhrmann film). While much of the dialog in the two films is the same, the different settings impact how the action of the story is presented and plays out.

As you are crafting the setting for your story, here are three things to keep in mind:

1. **Where** does the action of the story occur?
2. **When** does the action of the story occur?
3. **How** will the setting of the story be presented?

These are the questions you will need to address as you write your story. Depending on how you answer the *where* and the *when*, you may need to modify some of the elements you place in your story. For example, if you decide to set a story in what is now the American Southwest but set the story in the twelfth century, this will impact which objects you can include in your story. Answering the *how* will determine the style of narration you choose to present your story.

Finally, keep in mind that the setting is the stage on which your story plays out. Although an important part of your story, your setting should not overwhelm the action in the story. You should use the action and dialog in your story to help reveal the setting.

Choosing the setting wisely and following your decisions will help you create a winning story.

Reflection Questions

1. Using the "present day" as the setting for a story can make it easier for you to establish the setting for your story. What are some of the issues that you may have to risk as you write the story?

2. Assume you are planning to write a Science Fiction story that is set on the moon.

    a. What are some of the restrictions that the moon would place on your story?

    b. How would you have your narrator introduce these restrictions as your story progresses?

3. You decide to write a short story about your childhood memories of Christmas. Generally, you will want to center the story around your perceptions of that Christmas. Would you use first-person narration? Why?

4. You are writing a historical story set in the American Mid-West at the time of the Viet Nam War. (1960 – 1975).

   a. What differences in how you communicate might you need to address?

   b. Could any of these differences be ignored? For example, would you need to describe advances in telephone technology (cell phone vs landline)?

The Plot's the Thing!

By: Rebecca Fegan

"All the World's a Stage..."

~William Shakespeare

When we tell a story, we are attempting to put our audience in that particular place, at that particular time, in that particular circumstance. The characters going into the story are not the same coming out. Neither is the audience.

The Plot is what gets them from point A to point B. From being unaware of their gifts, resourcefulness, and creativity, to full awareness that allows them to save the day.

What if they don't need to "save the day" but just get the missing ingredients for the salsa from the grocery store? What if all they need to do is finish the project for the county fair, or find the missing pet?

Starting Small

In every story you tell or write, there must be a purpose for the story to exist. It can be to make new material or knowledge available to the audience. It could serve as a cautionary tale so the audience will not make the same mistakes and get into trouble. It might bring new awareness and consciousness to the listeners or readers that changes their perspective.

"When my mom was teaching beginners how to read music, they had problems learning the names of the lines on the treble and bass clef. She used words to stand for the letters, so treble clef lines were EGBDF, Elephants Got Big Dirty Feet! Bass clef lines were GBDFA, Great Burritos Don't Fall Apart. One of her students, a smart kid with a large vocabulary, put them together:

Great Burritos Don't Fall Apart, Coincidentally, Elephants Got Big Dirty Feet. Accident? (I think not!)"

Is this a story? No, this is an anecdote. It has no plot. It introduces new knowledge and a way to remember it, but it doesn't involve the student in the discovery. The thing that separates anecdotes and stories is **conflict.** There are many such conflicts we can observe:

There is External Conflict:
- Person vs One character
- Person vs Society
- Person vs Nature
- Person vs Supernatural
- Person vs Technology

The conflict we cannot observe is Internal, and that is:

- Person vs Self

External Conflict revolves around something or someone that physically keeps the protagonist from their goal.

For example, in every action movie, there is a protagonist and an antagonist, the Wicked Witch vs. Dorothy, Harry Potter vs. Voldemort, Ahab vs. Moby Dick... These are single-entity antagonists.

Though the protagonist may assemble a team to aid in overcoming the challenges put forth by the antagonist, when it comes to the final battle, it's one-on-one. The emotions and situations become very personal, and that results in a battle of wills.

But then there's a bigger picture, the person vs society. The protagonist is still the main force, but the opponent is a group of people. Examples would be Brave New World, Barbie in the Barbie movie, and Neo in the Matrix. The protagonist needs a team as well, but the challenge is too big to be faced by a single person.

The Person vs. Nature is a very popular conflict when looking at apocalyptic stories like "Into Thin Air" about the climb to the summit of Mount Everest, "Robinson Crusoe" where it's Crusoe and Friday against the island, and "The Edge" where people crash land in Alaska and are discovered by a man-eating bear. And, to be sure, we cannot forget Gilligan's Island.

Some of the most innovative stories are those of a Person vs. the Supernatural. The supernatural can represent a god, a ghost, a supervillain, or even an alien not unlike the Marvel and DC movies. Some of these stories are based on comic book characters, but there are those horror movies that have stood the test of time. The stories of Stephen King come to mind. Others include zombies, vampires, and all types of mythical creatures. These are great examples of Person vs. Supernatural. There was even a (really) long-running series called "Supernatural" based on this type of conflict.

A branch of the Person vs. Supernatural is a Person vs. Technology. Remember the talking computer, HAL, in "2001: A Space Odyssey"? The Borg in "Star Trek: The Next Generation" served in that capacity. "Jurassic Park" was a combination of three of these types of conflict: Person vs. Nature, Person vs. Supernatural nature, and Person vs. Technology with huge consequences. Nearly all of the zombie movies start with a technological aspect that goes awry. If you want the original zombie, don't forget "Frankenstein" by Mary Shelley.

Stories to inform

If you read the *story* of the discovery of Penicillin, you learn something about how scientific discoveries are made, the name of one of the Nobel prize winners, and see that this information is presented as facts with a plot.

"Dr. Fleming was experimenting with different molds to discover what antibacterial properties the molds had. He was on vacation and when he came back, he and his research scholar, Merlin Pryce, discovered that the bacteria in one of them had all but stopped reproducing near some mold that had contaminated that dish. He'd left the lid off and had not put the dishes into an incubator. If, instead, he had put all the dishes into the incubator, it might have been years before they discovered the properties of penicillin. But instead, he saved countless lives in World War II and won a Nobel Peace Prize." This involved a conflict of a person vs. nature.

It's a short story but it is effective because now when it's presented, it allows the reader or listener to hypothesize what he had discovered. It would be difficult to put this story into a two-hour movie. Let's examine the plot.

A. Introduced the main player and the object of his quest

B. The main player leaves an experiment for his assistant to work on, but it gets contaminated.

C. The research scholar and the main player determine the unique properties of the contaminant and make strides toward making an antibiotic that would kill certain bacteria and prevent infection.

D. The main player gets a Nobel prize.

Stories as a cautionary tale

Aesop's fables play a big role in this format. These stories have a plot and characters with a limited backstory, but they also include a moral. Don't put all your eggs in one basket. Don't put the cart before the horse. A bird in the hand is worth two in the bush.

The characters in a story like this can be caricatures or archetypes. They can be a more gentle way of introducing the "foolish person" by embodying him as an animal. In Aesop's story of the turtle and the scorpion, the scorpion stung the turtle knowing that the shell would protect it. The turtle, in turn, drowned the scorpion for its treachery. Character vs character-type conflicts help bolster the moral of the story.

There are cautionary tales we tell when we present some of our misadventures on vacation. There was the story I told about the time Dad didn't ask for directions and instead of finding Zion Canyon, we found ourselves on an Air Force firing range. Did I mention we were traveling in a big black car that looked like it should have had flags and diplomatic plates?

One of my favorite stories involves the words, "Trust us, we're professionals." It was a tale chronicling the events surrounding my broken hip in an Orlando Hotel at a Leadership summit.

The plots of these stories are succinct and directly to the point I am trying to make. There are no sub-plots and no extraneous characters. The conflicts exist but they're not very complex.

The format for these plots is also simple:

   A. The setting is revealed so we know what the conflict is.

   B. The main character and maybe a few others are introduced and a plan evolves.

   C. Details about the actions and reactions of the main character and the conflict emerge.

   D. Lesson learned.

Stories that bring awareness

Stories of this sort are not usually as simple since awareness is a more complex concept. These would encompass the plots to the Hallmark Holiday movies as well as the teaching series employed by John C. Maxwell. In one of his chapters in "The 21 Irrefutable Laws of Leadership", he talks about influence and tells a story of an influencer that had a profound effect on the congregation he was working with. His story about Claude expertly makes his point that "Leadership is Influence, Nothing More, Nothing Less." It brings awareness to future leaders on the role one plays in the marketplace, the workplace, or the family. This is primarily a conflict based on a Person vs. Self, though it has elements of other conflicts within the story.

The purpose of delving into the Person vs. Self is to aspire to a new level of consciousness, and often that takes place when a person Unlearns a habitual belief or traditional perspective.

Case in point: Have you ever gone to work and arrived not remembering a single moment of the journey? Have you made an assumption based on nothing more than habit?

There is a commercial where a couple meets a "financial professional" who represents a particular company in a commercial. They ask him what he does outside the working hours. They are assuming that at least occasionally, he wears a t-shirt and jeans and barbecues with his family in the back yard. He has no idea what they're talking about. This commercial illustrates, with humor, the assumption that the icons in the marketing campaigns are real people that have nothing else in life besides representing that company.

The biggest picture of plot is one that involves multiple characters, scenes, sub-plots, and makes use of many conflicts to multiple purposes. As merely an example:

- Raising Awareness in the hero
- Vanquishing an enemy for the greater good
- Building up of other members of the party
- Expanding the view of the world in its audience

It is the Hero's Journey.

The Hero's Journey
The great stories involve someone who might be considered "the reluctant hero." This is a person who is ill-prepared for his part in the adventure: He is missing the skills, the life experience, the contacts, the mind power, whatever is critical to accomplishing a goal.

Remember the last scene in the Wizard of Oz movie? Although the Scarecrow had intelligence all along, he just needed a diploma to prove it to himself. The Tin Man already had emotions; he just needed a heart with a heartbeat to remind him of this. The lion already had the courage, and Dorothy already had her way home. In this way, the characters became aware of their strengths and prowess. But they had to overcome some dire consequences to make use of their talents, skills, courage, and heart when it really mattered.

One model of this plot structure is called the Hero's Journey. Now in many models of the Hero's Journey, the basic plot device in most myths and adventures, you will see the path as circular. But in a really good story, the hero cannot return to his old life because he's not the same person who occupied that space before. It becomes more of a spiral.

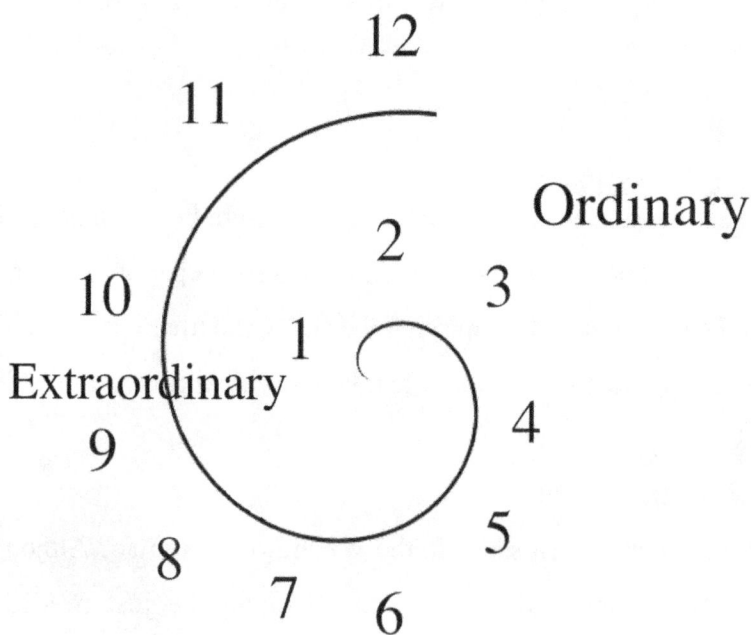

1. **The call to action.** The protagonist is presented with a situation that demands action. Dorothy's house is taken by the tornado to the land of Oz and she begins her odyssey home.

2. **Refusal of the call.** The protagonist resists the call initially. He or she decides to fulfill the quest due to the values they hold dear and their strength of character. Bilbo looks at his empty house and the contract, then he decides he must join the troop because it's the right thing to do.

3. **Meeting the Mentor.** Before the hero can accomplish the task, he has to meet a mentor or guardian who has pledged to help him and his teammates accomplish this goal. Harry Potter meets Dumbledore, the headmaster of the school.

4. **Crossing the Threshold.** This is the point where the protagonist moves from the ordinary and familiar to the extraordinary and dangerous. Dorothy starts on the Yellow Brick Road.

5. **Initial tests and trials.** In this part of the journey, the protagonist collects followers, and the antagonist is clarified. Each test reveals a strength or a weakness in the protagonist, his team, and the antagonist. The protagonist's team discovers how to work together. With 11 dwarves who all know each other and Gandalf the Grey, the wizard, whom everyone in the party knows, the only unknown asset is Bilbo. They have to build trust and rapport to work with each other. When Bilbo surprisingly rescues the rest of the party from the Trolls, he establishes himself among the group.

6. **The approach to the final conflict.** This is not the actual attack but the preparation for the attack. Coming to terms with the real risks of failure, the consequences of not going into the battle at all, the feeling of inadequacy and doubt, and the emotional examination. How do the hero and his party put aside fear and be willing to sacrifice their lives, sanity, or happiness for the greater good?

It's the final conversation before the battle of the Five Armies in the Hobbit, the fear the company feels when approaching the Wicked Witch's castle to rescue Dorothy, the realization that the only thing that spares the school is the death of Voldemort's snake and

Harry's ability to fight Voldemort though his followers were convinced Harry had died. This is usually the most emotional point the story and requires the characters and the audience to wonder what they would do in a situation similar to this.

Not all conflicts with antagonists end in life-threatening scenarios. The hero of "Mrs. Doubtfire" was fighting for a relationship with his family.

7. **The ordeal.** This could be the grand melee, the debate, the court case, or the championship game. It is here that the protagonist and his team go against the antagonist and his minions and require every bit of resourcefulness, creativity, specialized talents or tools, and determination they've accumulated on the journey to survive this conflict. Teammates may not survive. Injuries may be sustained. Sacrifices will be made. This is acutely recognized in the Battle of Hogwarts—the grand melee where all of Voldemort's followers fight the faculty and students of the school, and some of the most beloved die. In Romeo and Juliet, both our protagonists die!

8. **The hard-won reward.** This would be the pot of gold at the end of the rainbow. For Dorothy, it was the ability

to go home to Kansas. For Harry Potter, it was the ultimate defeat of the villain who killed his parents and threatened both the wizarding world and the non-magical world. For Bilbo, it was the end of the Dragon, the return of the dwarves to their homeland, and the re-establishment of peaceful relations among the races. It serves to release the long-building tension in the story, but it is not the end of the story.

9. **The return home.** After the ordeal, they are still in the territory of their enemies even though they have been vanquished. The party or parties head for home, but it is not without challenges. At this point, because of the growth of the characters during the first part of the journey, these challenges cement the approach to problems, the reliance on new-found friends, and their comfort in the new roles they have assumed. It serves to show them that some of the most harrowing situations they found themselves in were not nearly as scary as what they faced later. It further points out their starting place to show them how far they've come in their development.

10. **Transformation or Rebirth.** At this point in the story, the hero realizes how far he has come and acknowledges the changes—good and bad. Dorothy wakes up in her

bed and discovers a new appreciation for the people in her life. Harry Potter has experienced the death of friends, an epic battle with Voldemort, risking his life to rescue people who had plotted to kill him, and the ultimate power of possession of all three Deathly Hallows and has chosen to break the Elder Wand (the most powerful wand) to prevent it from falling into anyone else's hands.

11. **The return.** The hero and his party return to their lives, changed and more aware with new skills and insight. They may become less prone to turn down a new adventure, however.

12. **Conclusion…**or sequel? They live happily ever after but on a higher plane of existence. They fade away to the afterlife and true peace. They sit in their easy chairs with an enigmatic smile on their faces.

In this view of the plot, the main character begins in his familiar surroundings, with his familiar group of friends, his familiar work, and his expectations. He knows what he needs to know to maintain his status quo, and he feels comfortable with his skills and experiences. After his adventure, he's overqualified for his previous existence.

There was a World War II-era song called, "How you gonna keep'em down on the farm after they've seen Paris?" Soldiers returning from war found they could not inhabit the life they left. Women who'd never been in the industrial world were thrown into the physical labor pool and then shooed away when the soldiers came home. They couldn't resume their former lives. When we write or tell stories, sometimes we forget that after you slay the dragon, you can't go back to being a wheelwright or the baker anymore. You have a new reality, and so do the people inhabiting your stories as well as your audience.

But at the core of every story, it comes down to the conflict within the hero or his party. Nearly every Marvel movie that has characters from other realms (Spiderman plus Iron Man plus Thor...) includes a section where the characters jostle for position in the hierarchy or have grave philosophical differences. They must conclude that the antagonist may very well be smarter, more skilled, or more powerful than each of them, but he cannot be better than all of them together.

The reason for this is simple. If the hero comes in, saves the day, and then goes home, then he is a robot—a tool to be used to enhance society. It's why they introduce supervillains, apocalyptic worlds, and insane robots. A hero who steps in to solve ordinary problems appears to be a bully to enforce good behavior. People eventually revolt against a bully.

100

There is one scene in a Superman movie, "Man of Steel", where the government arrests him and takes him into an interrogation room, ***and he goes voluntarily!*** He has to turn himself in to General Zod to protect humanity. Unless he faces Zod, who is from Superman's home planet, and reconciles his alliance with humanity, there is no victory.

A hero who doesn't grow beyond his current state is no hero. Pinnochio becomes a real boy. Mrs. Doubtfire becomes the kind of dad his family needs. The Marvel heroes defeat Thanos. Dorothy appreciates her family. Harry becomes a wise father and the head Auror who seeks out those practicing dark magic. In a way, the stories we tell are an inspiration to grow beyond our self-limiting beliefs and become more aware and more conscious of the world around us. To do this, we take our listeners or readers on a journey they can look at concerning their mental, physical, and emotional growth.

How do we do that?

How to build a plot
We can start with the framework of our stories. But one thing becomes immediately clear: The hero's journey is difficult to shoehorn into a five-minute speech. The good news is that you do not have to use every single element in your story.

We think of the story in three parts: the opening, the body, and the close.

In the opening, we catch people's attention, explain the purpose of the story, and introduce our main character.

In the body, we show the audience the conflict, the process, and the outcome.

In the closing part, we summarize the main points and then the application of the message we hope to impart to our audience.

To do this, we decide what our main message is to be, then find a story to fit the message. There are some great ways to find stories in Mark's chapter and a wonderful demonstration of the difference between writing and presenting in Janel's chapter.

Some of us just collect stories and put them in a file. John C. Maxwell has a card file filled with stories divided into subject matter. Lance Miller (a Toastmasters International World Champion of Public Speaking Winner) keeps his old speeches.

Something to remember when writing stories for speeches is that the shorter the speech, the more succinct the language, and the more clear you need to make the point. If you are using stories to teach, you use one story to illustrate one point. You tell your story, explain why it was important to you, and how it affected your life or your perspective.

If you have a story in mind for the Great American Novel, you need to keep track of the story arcs. The background of the main characters has to be consistent, and the movement from the beginning of the story to the end needs to flow.

There is an axiom to remember: if you introduce a description of an aspect of one of the characters or a specific object you find in the room, you must make use of that knowledge. It is known as the Chekov's gun axiom. If there was a gun described in a Chekov story, it was going to go off. (You can find out more about Chekov's gun in Randy's chapter on Suspense.) If you mention one of the characters has a proclivity for close-up magic tricks, it has to be put into play at a critical juncture.

Scenes need to support the plot
In designing story arcs, remember that not all the characters will grow at the same rate. There is one place in the "Infinity War" movie where Bruce Banner cannot get mad enough to turn into the Incredible Hulk. This comes at a point where it is critical to the story, and everyone but Banner seems to have reached their peak performance physically and as a team.

Think of it like this: If you're in a classroom with a lot of other students, for some of them, the work required is not all that strenuous, and for others it's like climbing Mt. Everest. Not every scene in your plot will develop the characters in the same way or at the same rate.

Look at the Lord of the Rings. For the first part of their journey, the Hobbits, having rarely traveled out of the Shire are like fish out of water. They're on their first day of traveling, and they ask about Second Breakfast because they are not familiar with long-distance travel and the need to set a pace fast enough to avoid enemies, but this is second nature to Stryder and Gandalf.

Early in the story, during the fight scenes, the Hobbits mostly run and hide, but in the final battle, they are fully armed and armored, fighting side-by-side with their friends.

In a speech, you want to pick out the scenes from your story that focus on the growth of your main character. What new skill does he/she reveal or develop? What types of emotional trials must be faced to bring them to their new selves?

Your plot is the structure of your story
Your plot must support your message and needs to be examined for consistency and logic. It's one reason that many speakers write the speech or the story and then add the title. But if you

have an agenda you wish to get across, especially if you don't know your audience well enough to call on shared experiences, the story brings them all to the same conclusion. From there you can make your pitch, your plea, your goal.

You might think of your plot as the bulletin board with all the characters, places, and events pinned to it and connected with red strings. (Why red? Because if you have photographs and newspaper clippings, the red doesn't get lost and fade into the background.)

Think of your readers as investigators. Can they arrive at the same end of the story you wrote, or do they get tangled up and eaten by giant spiders? If your plot becomes too convoluted, the reader or listener may stop listening because it appears that the presenter (be it in book form or orally performed) is just rambling on without a purpose. If it is straightforward but lacks suspense (see Randy's chapter), humor, or surprise, they nod off and never read or hear the ending.

Some writers do an outline for the story, then smaller outlines for the chapters. World Champion speakers have outlines for their speeches because they are masters of the short forms of stories. Some of their stories can be measured in less than one and a half minutes or even mere seconds!

But long or short, dramatic or humorous, written or told, your stories will depend on a plot. The more familiar you are with it, the better your stories will be.

Reflection Questions

Your homework! Read some short stories, and note the plot.

1. In your favorite stories, what about the plot keeps you interested all the way to the end?

2. If there are stories you hate, what keeps you from enjoying them?

3. In longer stories, such as movies, how does the hero's journey appear? Is it a full journey or abridged?

4. In speeches, the presenter will often use stereotypes for minor characters. What advantages would that process have?

5. What is it about a good story that makes a listener or reader suspend their disbelief?

Use of Suspense in a Story

By: Randy Prier

"This suspense is terrible. I hope it will last."

~Oscar Wilde

". . .but a singular sense of impending calamity,
that should indeed have served me as a
warning, drove me onward."

"The Time Machine

~H.G. Wells

Introduction

Have you ever picked up a book and started to read only to find that you can't put it down? You stay up all night until you finish. Or perhaps you're the kind who skips to the last chapter because you just can't wait to find out "whodunit." Dollars to donuts the reason is that the author has done a masterful job of building suspense to a fever pitch. The twists and turns in the plot keep you nailed to your chair (or in bed with the light on). Suspense is a literary device that adds interest and excitement. In this chapter we explore the use of this device in storytelling.

Suspense Defined

Suspense can be defined as a feeling of anxious uncertainty about what may happen in the story. Suspense happens when the reader is on the edge of a pivotal moment, and they don't know what's going to happen next. Writers can create suspense by carefully withholding and releasing information to the reader as the plot progresses. All writers should try to work suspense into their stories because that's what keeps readers engaged. If you have skillfully built the suspense, your readers cannot help themselves, they must know what happens. But it doesn't have to involve frantic car chases or lurking psychopaths stalking the hero/heroine. There can be suspense in everything from a tense corporate boardroom meeting to a teenager's trials in a coming-of-age story. In other words, lives don't have to be at stake. You, as the author, can generate suspense out of relatively mundane things as long as they are important to the story.

Suspense could further be described as like being on a roller coaster. The trip up to the top is the suspense, and the fast trip down the hill is the outcome or pay-off. But you want to make sure the climax lives up to the suspense. If you've written yourself to the top of the roller coaster but have yet to fashion the climax, ask yourself, what would interest, shock, or shake your reader? Think of your characters. Do they have enough obstacles, and are they reacting in character to what happens? Did the villains get an appropriate comeuppance?

Methods to build suspense:

1. Create suspense using time constraints.

Imposing a time limit for your characters to discover something or solve a problem is one of the most effective ways to build tension and suspense. In the TV series "24" from several years ago, each episode revolved around some challenge that US government agents had to solve within one day in order to avoid some kind of international calamity. Maybe it was a plot to assassinate a world leader that had to be foiled or important information to be uncovered before a crucial international conference. By giving them a ticking clock, the writers gave viewers a sense of the limitations the series characters faced that made their efforts even more urgent. If you find yourself struggling with a flat scene, see if you can impose a time limit on your characters. This will heighten the suspense for the reader and give the characters a new dynamic.

2. Create suspense with character flaws.

All your characters should have both strengths and weaknesses that readers can identify with. The whole array of human experience is available to you, from addiction to poor choices in love. You create suspense by showing the way your characters deal with their weaknesses. Your readers will understand the battles happening in the character's mind and the dangers they're facing. Each such example raises a dramatic question for the reader: will the protagonist succumb to their weakness, or will they be strong enough to resist? What will the outcome be? The details you add hold the readers' attention as they wait to find out.

3. Create suspense with cliffhangers.

A cliffhanger raises a big, dramatic question that leaves the reader hanging. It's one of the most effective ways to create suspense, but don't use it too often, the reader can grow desensitized. The classic cliffhanger puts your character(s) in danger, like being caught in an avalanche or on a railroad track with a train bearing down. Did they survive? If so, how did they escape? But a cliffhanger could also involve your character being given a heart-rending choice, then moving the narrative away into a new scene before the reader finds out which way the character chose. They'll have to keep reading to find out!

4. Create suspense with foreshadowing.

Foreshadowing is a literary device that lays clues for what's to come later in the story. It's a more subtle, slow-burn kind of suspense. Readers familiar with story structure know that everything in a story happens for a reason. They will hang on throughout the story to see how the foreshadowed element fits. The movie producer/director Alfred Hitchcock was known as a master of suspense, especially including foreshadowing. His masterpiece, "Psycho," is full of dramatic foreshadowing that is, at the same time, misleading. First of all, the movie is in the horror genre of suspenseful stories, just without aliens or grotesque monsters. The mood of the movie is set from the beginning by being shot in stark black and white with jarring, dramatic music. This in itself foreshadows the dark happenings that are to come.

Marion's flight from her crime, the creepy house up the hill from the motel she stops at, strange voices coming from the house, the actions of the nervous young manager of the motel all foreshadow that something dramatic and shocking is coming. Yet, even with all the foreshadowing, we are unprepared for the shower scene and the even more unexpected ending of the movie. I was 14 when I saw the movie with my parents during its first theatrical showing, and I still remember the fascination and foreboding I felt while watching it. I was apprehensive because I knew something terrible was going to happen, but I couldn't turn away.

Your foreshadowing, however, doesn't need to be so dramatic. You can use it to establish expectations for the story. For example, you could open with a reminiscence: "At my wedding, I danced with two people: the one I married, and the one I should have married." The reader then spends the entire story wondering which is which. What caused the narrator to marry the wrong one? This foreshadowing reveals the outcome, but not how you arrive there. This creates suspense as the reader waits for bits and pieces to make the path come clear.

However, while being highly effective in creating suspense, foreshadowing is one of the easiest elements to mess up. As a writer you know how everything is going to turn out. So, it's all too easy to drop hints thinking you're being subtle and clever. But if you're not careful, the hints can be as subtle as a piano falling on your reader's head. This is the sort of foreshadowing done in many soap operas and movies. The joke is that when a soap opera character gets a stomachache, you can count on him soon winding up in critical care.

On the other hand, sometimes the hints are so vague that the only person who "gets" them is the author. For example, in a story about a character who is slowly being poisoned, the author might carefully research the symptoms of arsenic poisoning, including pain in the hands and feet. Then the writer gives those symptoms to his character, forgetting that most readers don't know that those are symptoms of arsenic poisoning. So, when the character starts having trouble walking because of the pain in the soles of his feet, the readers are confused about what happened. Foreshadowing should not make readers go "What?" or "Huh?"

Finally, sometimes the problem is that there is no foreshadowing. Everything is going along, and BOOM, a character does or says something outrageous, without any precedent, like turning into a psychotic stalker. As said earlier, characters need to have a reason for the things they do. Clever foreshadowing can give readers the hints they need.

5. Create suspense with dramatic irony.

Dramatic irony happens when the reader knows more about what's happening than the characters do. This is a mainstay of the horror genre. You show the reader that the killer is hiding behind the door, then show the protagonist moving closer and closer to the door. Alternatively, a chance happening causes some key information to go astray. (See another Alfred Hitchcock movie *North by Northwest*, where the simplest misidentification at the beginning leads to a wild run of misadventures.) Misunderstandings and shenanigans ensue. Suspense arises as the reader waits to see how the story's characters will react to the misinformation and how they'll finally come together.

Additional Tips for Effective Use of Suspense

- **Avoid contrived suspense.**

How many movies have you seen, or stories read where something like this happens: The heroine walks into a parking garage all alone even though there's a serial killer stalking her? Characters need a reason to act in a certain way. Most people in mortal danger will want to find an answer rather than running around in a deserted house or other creepy place. In the same vein, you don't want to throw in random obstacles that don't stem from the plot or characters. Say your hero is trying to get away from murderous drug dealers. He runs across a parking lot and almost gets runover, so has to stop. Or when he gets to his car, he can't find his keys. These obstacles might seem exciting, but instead of relying on random problems, why not use your villains to make your hero's life harder? Have them damage his car, forcing him to find another way to get away. That's more interesting than a bumbler who suddenly can't find his keys.

- **Avoid false suspense.**

For example, the story makes you think something important is about to happen, only to find out the "prowler" turns out to be the heroine's cat. Or the frontier heroine thinks she hears a wild animal growling outside and scratching at the door, only to discover it was the hero's dog. I was not a reader of Nancy Drew books, but I understand that every chapter ended with something shocking. For example, Nancy would hear footsteps coming up the stairs in the middle of the night. The excited reader would turn the page to the next chapter, only to learn that it was her father, coming home late. Don't inflict scenes like this on your audience. Too many "false alarms," and readers will give up on you.

- **Suspense should come out of the characters as well as the plot.**

If you're not comfortable with the ways your characters are acting, maybe there's a logic hole in the plot. But it could also be that your characters need some work. Spend some time figuring out how characters react to suspense, anxiety, and fear. (For more information about character development and the use of character sheets, see Chapter 5, "Crafting Characters for Your Stories," by Rebecca Fegan.) A good way to start is by thinking about how you felt the last time something scary or stressful happened to you. Did you get a knot in your stomach, did you shriek or swear, or did you just calmly handle the situation then break down later? Remember, not everyone reacts the same way.

For that matter, not all suspenseful situations are the same. The brave cop who is calm and collected in a shootout might feel his stomach clench when he has to give a talk to a hall full of highschoolers. In any case, when you write about the situation, try to avoid trite descriptions like "her pulse raced." Use mood to evoke suspense. Movie makers have a lot of tools, print writers don't. They can play spooky or dramatic music, change the lighting, have the actors look scared or worried, and use many other effects to generate suspense. Writers have to stick to words, but words can be extremely powerful tools. Just look at Edgar Allen Poe's "The Tell Tale Heart." See how Poe skillfully uses the protagonist's own self-talk to describe his gradual descent into madness driven by guilt and the imagined continued beating of his victim's heart. Just remember that one writing style doesn't work for every writer, nor does the same style work for every scene. While terse, concise terms and choppy sentences are appropriate in many situations, if you can make a florid writing style work, go for it. Just remember that sometimes the most suspenseful writing style is one that doesn't get in the way at a crucial moment.

- **Don't make things too easy for your hero or heroine.** If they find information they need too easily, that takes away some of the suspense. Give them some obstacles to work through. For a masterfully suspenseful example of obstacles overcome by grinding detective work, check out novelist Frederick Forsyth's book, *The Day of the Jackal* (and its 1973 film adaptation). Based on actual events, the story follows the attempts by French and British officials to first identify and then thwart the efforts of a contract killer to assassinate French President Charles de Gaulle in 1962. The twists and turns are too many to describe here, but the story will keep you rapt to the very end. You may not be up to constructing such complex plots, but the novel may give you some ideas on how to throw obstacles in your protagonists' way.

- **When suspense is involved, real life should intrude**.

While much of the action in *The Day of the Jackal* was made up, it is historical fiction based on gritty, real events in 1960s Europe. Adding plenty of real-life details will make the suspense feel closer to home. Getting back to our heroine running away from a stalker, maybe hearing a radio playing "Every Breath You Take" by the Police, concentrates her thoughts about the stalker. She should be present in a concrete world, full of material things we can relate to--the sights and smells of the street, her shoes which are too tight, etc. Such small details will be more noticeable when our heroine is worried—just as when you're stressed at work, you can suddenly overhear every conversation, microwave beep, printer and building noise you hear.

Plot Devices Used in Evoking Suspense

Chekov's Gun:

Anton Chekov was a 19th Century Russian playwright and short story author. In commenting on the art of creating stories, he wrote, "If you say in the first chapter that there is a rifle hanging on the wall, in the second or third chapter it absolutely must go off. If it's not going to be fired, it shouldn't be hanging there." Basically, Chekhov's Gun is a narrative principle that if the audience's attention is drawn to some kind of element in great detail, that element should be necessary in the overall story, i.e., if the writer hadn't included it, it wouldn't be important. Writers should not bother with details that aren't significant. Chekhov, of course, perfectly used the plot device that now bears his name in his most well-known play, "The Seagull." The main character carries a gun around at the beginning of the play, and by the end has used that same gun to commit suicide.

Chekov's Gun can be an element of foreshadowing but is technically not the same thing. Foreshadowing involves hints that something is going to happen, while an actual Chekhov's Gun can be anything at all—a gun, a bottle of pills, a scent, a backstory about a character's evil twin brother—anything that will be brought up again later in the story with significance.

To use the Chekov's Gun principle effectively, scan your story to make sure you haven't included a detail or piece of information that doesn't end up being important by the end. If it's not important, it's probably best to leave it out. Be careful though, attempts to use this plot device can easily go wrong. Sometimes a Chekhov's Gun is fired without it being loaded (no setup) or loaded without ever being fired (no payoff), both of which leave audiences disappointed. But when used skillfully, a Chekhov's Gun can add an additional layer to the story's overall meaning. From how they present the "gun" to the audience to how fast or slow it is fired, to how important it seems to the plot — the best writers will use various elements of the Chekhov's

Gun principle to spin the plot device on its head and make their storytelling even better.

Well known examples of the use of the Chekov's Gun principle include Charles Foster Kane's sled in Orson Welles' movie Citizen Kane, and Q's briefings at the beginning of every James Bond movie on the latest spy craft gadgets, at least one of which will save Bond's life.

Peripeteia and Anagnorisis:

Peripeteia is a literary term referring to an unexpected reversal of circumstances or a sudden change of fortune in a story. Storytellers use this literary device in the form of plot twists and key turning points that lead a story to its resolution. Peripeteia alters the course of a story and impacts the well-being of the main character. The classic example of this device is in Sophocles' Greek tragedy, "Oedipus Rex," when Oedipus discovers he is the one prophesied who unknowingly killed his father and married his mother. The revelation leads to Oedipus gouging out his eyes in grief and complete demoralization.

Anagnorisis, which is closely related to peripeteia, is a literary term for a moment of recognition or revelation in a story. Storytellers use anagnorisis in recognition scenes when the main character finally comprehends the true nature of a situation or his own character. In the movie *The Sixth Sense*, anagnorisis occurs when Malcolm Crowe, a child psychologist treating a boy who can see and talk to the dead, realizes that he himself is dead. Another example occurs in *Star Wars* when Darth Vadar reveals himself as Luke Skywalker's true father.

If one or both of these elements are skillfully set up, using the techniques described above to generate suspense, the pages will fly by.

Conclusion

Whatever type of book or short story you write, keeping your readers in suspense will ensure that they keep turning the pages. You just might write the book that makes their humdrum weekend livable. But you must carefully construct your story using the various techniques outlined in this chapter to create the suspense. And if you're good enough, maybe you'll keep them reading even when it's sunny out and the chores are all done.

Reflection Questions

1. Read a sampling of suspenseful books by authors such as Agatha Christie, Tom Clancy, Frederick Forsyth, or other mystery/action/adventure writers to see how they do it. What writing styles and tricks did the authors use to create suspense?

2. Try your hand at writing a short story using one or more of these techniques to create suspense: Time constraints; Character flaws; Cliffhangers; Foreshadowing; or Dramatic Irony. Did you find it easy or difficult? What was your favorite technique?

3. Peripeteia and Anagnorisis are obscure terms which you may not have heard of before. See if you can construct a situation which makes use of one or both of these plot devices to establish a dramatic, suspenseful conclusion to a story.

Point of View

By: Keith Jones

*"There is nothing insignificant in the world. It
all depends on the point of view."*
~ *Johann Wolfgang von Goethe*

Point of View

What makes a story strong? Whether we are reading a story or being captivated by a story being told to us, it is easy to forget the way in which it is being presented to us. Believable characters, engaging plots, or fascinating settings are all influenced by the point of view being used to tell the story. The secret of a successful story lies in the narrator's ability to tell the story from the right point of view.

There are several types of point of view; first-person, second-person, and third-person. Another perspective is fourth-person which is not used very often. Let us explore how point of view functions, which point of view a writer should use and, examples of each.

Point of View vs Perspective

Point of view and perspective are sometimes used interchangeably. Each refer to the characters and how we see the story. They give us a range of choices as to how we communicate with our reader. However, perspective and point of view are not quite the same thing.

What is "Point of View?" Point of view is the direction from which the story is being told and the way the writer chooses to communicate with the reader. In other words, it determines who is narrating the story.

Perspective has to do with the character's place in the world. We are told who the characters are, the way they see things and the way the world sees them. Stories will usually be told in one point of view, but have multiple perspectives.

Different Points of View

There are four different overarching point of view categories; first, second, third and fourth, with several point of view types within them.

First-person point of view is told from the perspective of the character, using the pronoun "I."

In a work of fiction, the narrator determines the story's point of view. If the narrator is a full participant in the story's action, the narrative is said to be in the first-person.

Second-person point of view is told from the perspective of the reader as a character, using the pronoun "you."

A third-person point of view story is told by the author or an external narrator who is not a character in the story. This perspective uses the pronouns "he," "she," or "they."

The fourth-person point of view is told from the perspective of everyone narrating the story using the pronoun "we."

Understanding the narrator's point of view strengthens writing and clarifies the story for the readers. Establishing this when a writer begins writing a story helps make good writing choices and avoid writing mistakes. A writer needs to consistently maintain a character's point of view throughout the story. Abrupt changes or mistakes within perspective distracts readers and increases their confusion during the reading of the story.

There are limitations in the amount of information an author can share with the reader in some points of view. With a first-person point of view, the main character can't understand other characters' motivations. Using a different point of view may expand the amount of information an author can convey and how to convey it. Third-person limited point of view means that no character's motivations may be crystal clear. Choosing a limited third-person point of view and sticking with it, limits the information an author can give the audience. Third-person unlimited may have the disadvantage of the reader not participating in the story.

Let's look at the different types of point of view and how they are used in writing.

First-Person Subjective

There are two types of first-person points of views in literature. Both are written as though the story is told by the central character. For example,

> *I closed the door behind me, as Grandma always told me, and walked down the stairs.*

This point of view makes the reader feel as though they are experiencing the world of the story right beside them.

Most first-person narratives are told in a subjective manner. It's as if the character might be writing in a journal or talking to a friend. The character's thoughts, feelings, and ideas are shown on the page.

For example,

> *I closed the door behind me, as Grandma always told*
> *me, and walked down the stairs. The excitement was*
> *building inside me at the thought of tasting the cool*
> *refreshing ice cream that was about to be made.*

The access to the narrator's inner thoughts and emotions are what made this point of view "subjective."

First-Person Objective

The first-person objective is a more removed point of view that can be used to great effect. It is characterized by showing the actions happening in the story. For example,

> *I closed the door behind me, as Grandma always told*
> *me, and walked down the stairs. Ice cream was going to*
> *be made.*

If the story has been developed leading up to this moment effectively, then that short, simple sentence might be enough to show everything the first-person narrator is going through.

This narrative style can be used very effectively in describing experiences without including emotions the characters are having. Events can be laid out in close detail allowing the reader to watch alongside the narrator like a video footage. This makes the story more real and more objective because the narrative is not being filtered through the narrator's inner thoughts and emotions.

Second-Person

What is second-person point of view? The second-person point of view stories are told from the perspective of the reader. Second-person point of view is characterized by the use of the word "you." It is the narrator talking directly to the reader and addressing them with that second-person pronoun. This is a story written so closely woven that the reader and the protagonist become one and the same. This is difficult to do well. This is generally better suited for short stories and not novels. Try writing a second-person point of view story to stretch your limits as a writer.

This narrative point of view is most often used in nonfiction writing (like this chapter), advertising copy, certain types of video games, blog posts, song lyrics, and self-help books.

Try this example,

> *You closed the door behind you, as Grandma always told you to, and started to walk down the stairs. The stairwell was dark. Can you find the light switch?*

This sets up even more tension, because you are now a part of the story. Right away the reader knows they are in for something very special. Second-person narration creates immersion in the story as though they were reading about themselves.

Then, unlike the protagonists of the first or third-person narration, who continue their story long after, your reader closes the book when they are finished, knowing that they lived something wonderful and now the adventure is complete.

Third-Person Limited Subjective

The main character in a third-person narrative is described with pronouns such as "he," "she," or "they." Stories in third-person point of view are from the view of a camera. If the camera moves in close and the focus is on one character, you might follow the thoughts of that one person. Third-person limited point of view means focusing on just one character, while third-person multiple or third-person omniscient means following many.

Third-person limited subjective is a subtype of the third-person narrative, and is quite similar to first-person subjective. This narrative follows the main character through the whole story and allows the reader to see what they are thinking and feeling in response to the world around them. This is a classic storytelling style that allows us to view the events of the story through the lens of a single character.

For example:

He closed the door behind him, as Grandma always told him, and walked down the stairs. His excitement was building inside him at the thought of tasting the cool refreshing ice cream that was about to be made.

Like with a first-person narrative, the reader may get access to the character's inner thoughts. The difference between the two points of view is that in the first-person point of view, the protagonist is telling us their own thoughts and feelings. In the third-person limited subjective point of view, an outside narrator, the camera, is telling us what the protagonist is thinking and feeling. This makes the third-person narrator less "subjective" than the first-person perspective.

Third-Person Multiple Subjective

This type of third-person point of view is like the third-person limited subjective point of view in that it can peer into the mind of a character. The difference is that third-person multiple subjective goes deeper into the thoughts and feelings of several characters, not just the protagonist.

This narrative style might explore all the central characters in a story, or only a selection of them, for example, alternating between two siblings. The crucial part of third-person multiple subjective point of view is that when a character comes in to focus, they become the center of that moment in the story, whether that moment is a scene, a chapter, or a longer "part one." In other words, we see thoughts and feelings of the third-person limited narrator, but not those of the other characters around them.

For example:

He closed the door behind him, as Grandma always told him, and walked down the stairs. His excitement was building inside him at the thought of tasting the cool refreshing ice cream that was about to be made. His cousin was impatiently waiting at the bottom of the stairs, for the container of mixture that would soon be made into ice cream. Jim was thinking "HURRY UP!" but did not want to startle him in case he dropped the mixture.

Third-Person Objective

The third-person objective point of view style most closely resembles the way we would see a story being played out on screen. We follow several characters throughout the course of the story, but only as an external observer. We see their actions, experiences, moments of joy and sadness, hear what they say out loud and see what they're communicating with their bodies, but never go any deeper into their consciousnesses. Think of the narrator as a camera: the narrator can only observe events and not be able to communicate any of the characters emotions.

For example:

Randy closed the door behind him, as Grandma always told him, and walked down the stairs. He was carrying the container filled with mixture for the cool refreshing ice cream that was about to be made. Jim, his cousin at the bottom of the stairs, was impatiently waiting for the container that would soon hold ice cream.

Third-Person Omniscient

Like third-person multiple subjective, the third-person omniscient point of view allows the reader to see into the minds of more than one character. The difference is that in an omniscient narration, it's all happening at once. We can watch a conversation between two characters unfold and know what each of them is saying, thinking, and not saying aloud. We'll know if someone in the next room is overhearing them and drawing conclusions of their own. And we'll know what every one of these people is planning to do next.

This format gives the writer a lot more freedom within the story. It's a godlike viewpoint that can relay information to the reader in more ways than any other commonly used point of view. For many writers this point of view is attractive especially if they are writing a book with lots of characters. This opens up a lot of possibilities but can limit intimacy between the reader and characters. The unlimited narrator can start a scene by describing the weather and landscape, then shift to a character in a windowless room, describing them and telling the reader what they are thinking about.

Third-person omniscient point of view is useful in creating a sense of suspense in the reader, as it shows us things that the protagonist doesn't yet know. An expert storyteller can use an omniscient narrator to reveal just enough that we understand the goals and motivations of several of the players on the stage, while still leaving us room to be surprised.

The unlimited narrator is not hampered by time or distance, either. So, the narrator can hint at things to come, even though there is no way any of the characters could know what lies ahead. A reader can often tell an unlimited narrator by the use of lines like: *"She had no way of knowing that things were about to get much worse."* Or: *"Waiting for her around the corner was the killer, looking for his tenth victim."* This is known as dramatic irony, and used in many third-person unlimited stories.

Any time the narrator shares some information that the characters could not know, it's a good bet the writer has written with a third-person unlimited point of view. Even if these little asides don't happen very often in the book.

Third-Person Omniscient Example:

It was a hot summer day. Grandma had just mixed the heavy cream, condensed milk, and vanilla extract into the container for the hand cranked ice cream bucket. She handed it to Randy and told him it was ready to take down stairs. Randy proceeded to the doorway to the basement door. He closed the door behind him, as Grandma always told him, and walked down the stairs. He was carrying the container filled with mixture that the cool refreshing ice cream that was about to be made. Jim, his cousin, at the bottom of the stairs, was impatiently waiting for the container that would soon boast ice cream.

One of the hallmarks of third-person unlimited is the ability to know multiple characters' thoughts, even in the same scene.

Fourth-Person
Fourth-person point of view is a newer writing style that's gathering steam as writers use it to explore big-picture social

questions. It's similar to first-person point of view in that it's told from the perspective of the character, only in this case the fourth-person narrative perspective is a collective group of people, or a representation of a group of people such as a social class. There are two types of fourth-person point of view, the collective "we" and "us" and the indefinite "one," "someone," or "anyone." For the purposes of storytelling, writers are more likely to use the collective one.

To illustrate this, here is first-person:

I closed the door behind me, as Grandma always told me, and walked down the stairs. The excitement was building inside me at the thought of tasting the cool refreshing ice cream that was about to be made.

Now in fourth-person:

One of us closed the door behind the group, as Grandma always told us, and together we walked down the stairs. The excitement was building inside all of us at the thought of tasting the cool refreshing ice cream that was about to be made.

No Wrong Way to Write

It is important to understand that there is no wrong point of view in storytelling. You need to be aware that your story can be very different depending on which point of view you choose. Writing from first-person or second-person can lead to immediacy and create intimacy with your readers. Writing in the third-person point of view allows more distance between the reader and the characters. The benefit of the third-person view offers the reader a more comprehensive view of the story world than the characters can see.

When starting a new story, try different points of view to see what will fit best with your reader. Challenge yourself to write from a different point of view than you usually write. Writers learn and grow by trying new techniques.

Mistake New Writers Make

Powerful and engaging stories can be created with any one of these points of view. But, once you have established the point of view for your story, you must stick with it. It is confusing to the reader when you slip from on point of view to another. The reader will stop mid page and toss the book into the trash if you jump from one point of view to another. Consistency is very important throughout your story. It is very easy to not be consistent. Hopefully you will catch this, or your editor will catch this when going over your work.

Which point of view will you choose?

The other question may be, "Which point of view is best for your story?" It may boil down to two things; what level of intimacy you want the reader to have with your character, and how much information you want them to have about what's happening in the story.

You may already be comfortable with one point of view in particular. You may choose this to tell your story. Or, you may challenge yourself and write in some form unfamiliar to you.

Another factor to consider is what genre you are writing in. Any point of view can be used in any genre, but some are more common than others.

For instance, in writing for young adults, first-person is the common point of view with third-person limited is a close second. For romance, first-person is most common followed by third-person limited. Epic fantasy is most commonly written in third-person limited, with some third-person omniscient. A mystery, a thriller, or a suspense story is written in third-person limited.

Whatever point of view you choose, make sure to read up on the conventions on that style, and read books written in it. This will greatly improve your writing and put you on the path toward success in your prose.

Conclusion

Point of view is one of the components of writing involved in creating your story. The more you write the more you will learn about all the components involved in good writing.

Like any craft form, writing is full of pieces that we need to maneuver into place to get the best out of our work. Point of view is one of these pieces that is an essential cog that quietly supports the other building blocks of our story and helps make them as powerful as they can be.

Our point of view style helps us engage readers with our characters, bring them into the world of our story, and manage the delicate balance of tension, revelation, and suspense. As you experiment with these different narrative styles, you'll see that a well-chosen point of view in your story can make all the difference.

Review Questions

1. Think of a short story of an incident that has happened to you. Write it down just to get the particulars on paper. Don't worry about what point of view just yet.

2. Take that story and write in in first-person point of view.

3. Take that same story and write it in second-person point of view

4. Take that same story and write it in third-person point of view

5. Pick up your favorite book and look at it to determine what point of view it has been used and how it impacts the story.

Verbosity

By: Christine Jones

"One of the big mistakes some doctoral candidates make is to assume that scholarly writing has to sound "scholarly."

"Usually, clear simple statements make for better writing no matter the audience. "I'd like to challenge all of you to review your comments just prior to submittal with the intent to simplify them."

"Ask yourself if the sentence can be expressed more simply. Are sentences lengthy? Do they contain multiple clauses? Could this be made more clear by splitting these sentences up or by omitting words?"

"When I create a first draft of writing, I try to do this. I have consistently found that 20 to 40% of the words I initially write are extraneous, convoluted, and confusing. I often go word by word and ask myself if the word is absolutely necessary. If I don't have a compelling reason to keep it, I omit.

"Of course, many of us scholars are long-winded to begin with, so this may not be surprising. But I will say that after I perform this exercise, my writing carries more punch, sounds more authoritative, and most importantly is clearly understood. "

"Dr. Wolff"

"P.S. Before submitting this comment, I omitted more than 50 words from the first draft."

~ Dr. Nick Wolff

Simplify Your Writing for Fun and Profit

Our word choices matter. That is why I am writing this chapter. Let's explore more about word choices.

As one who has had many discussions with Dr. Wolff, I have developed better writing skills. I have found that even with a college degree along with decades of life lived, I often use too many or too few words to get my point across. He has patiently worked with me to improve the balance of my verbiage.

Dr. Wolff works with doctoral candidates as they prepare their thesis submissions. While The Alternative Book Club writers are not among those, as colleagues in this group of writers, it is a constant learning experience as we seek to express our thoughts to you, the reader, clearly and concisely. (Yes, I have already rewritten these two paragraphs at least ~~five~~ eight times!)

I asked Dr. Wolff a few questions about the statements quoted above. "Is this framed in your office?"

"No, that's an excellent idea. I probably would be able to capture a couple of the key comments and put it on my wall."

"What was the purpose behind this post?"

"It's laid out pretty well that sometimes people are trying to sound scholarly. I had no intention other than I don't want people to sound scholarly. I want them to sound intelligent and make a point to do it concisely. This is a post to my doctoral candidates, telling them and imploring them to be more concise and clear in their writing and to not feel the need to use a lot of, as you say, verbose language to try and say what you want using simple clear words to convey meaning."

"Yes, Nick! That's what I'm looking for with these questions. I'm just looking for the shorter answers just to show a demonstration of "say what you mean" and say it in short order. How was it received?"

"For them, some people didn't care for it too much. However, I've had some people come to me at their graduation reception telling me 'Thank you for the comment.' They saw the value in it."

"How long did it take to write?"

"I wrote it in about 40 minutes. It didn't take long at all, but I did take about 10 min to revise it to get rid of all the extraneous words."

"Would you make any changes to it today?"

"I don't think so."

"Spell checker keeps trying to change 'more clear' into 'clearer.' Why did you say "more clear" rather than clearer?""

"I get that. I can see it going either way. Just to my ear, more clear sounds better in that context. Sometimes we can use one word, but it doesn't sound good to our ears. And that's the point I want to make regarding that question. What we hear when words are spoken can have a different sound to our ears."

"Thank you, Dr. Nick Wolff."

I find this to be a typical conversation where I leave feeling like I just had my mind stretched by my scholarly friend. Dr. Wolff has taught me to be cognizant of how verbosity impacts what I have to say. Keep your eyes open to see how our conversation impacted my writing this chapter!

Our word choices matter.

We Make Assumptions About Our Readers

As noted in Dr. Nick's quote and discussion above, there is a time when we need to sound scholarly and a time to demonstrate our intellect. He works with students pursuing their doctoral degrees which makes sounding intellectual appropriate. Scholarly writing may contain fancy verbiage. Intellectual writing shows that the author has an understanding of the material. The writing we do in this book series is directed to a more general audience. The difference in our purpose means that those scholarly or intellectual words may go over the tops of many of our heads. Nonetheless, we want to challenge your intellect as you read this collection. Should you encounter words that are perplexing to you, take the time to look them up. It will serve to expand your vocabulary which helps boost your intellect. It also serves as an example of how word choices matter.

With that perspective in mind, let's dig in!

We Just Like to Keep Rambling

It may seem like the first few pages of this chapter seem to be rambling. They do have a purpose! To get into our study, they need to set our scene as well as serve as reference material as we move forward. Now that we are on the same page, let's chat about rambling.

If you noticed, Dr. Wolff noted that he eliminated about fifty words within about ten minutes of editing his initial draft. He did that to cut out some rambling thus getting more to his point.

When I write now, I find myself just writing out my thoughts with whatever words come to mind at that moment. Sometimes, there are about ten words. Sometimes, it can take me twenty or thirty words just to say, "I do not know what to say about that." It can come out like, "That is something I will have to research in order to sound like at least some sort of intelligent person even though I have no clue about that subject." Yes, the second version is rambling although it does sound intellectual!

We Do Not Know What to Say That Makes Our Point

Finding the Right Words

We may know ~~that~~ we want to make a point. How do we find the words? Start with just noting your point no matter how rough it sounds. You may be surprised that you struggle because of a lack of self-confidence more than anything. I want you to know ~~that~~ what you have to say matters. Let it out! It is not necessary to write it out perfectly the first time. Like Dr. Wolff did, and I am doing now, write it out. Then, go back over it to see if it says what you want, the way that you want others to understand.

Once you begin to put your words down, what tools can you use to improve them? When I write, I have a dictionary and a thesaurus handy. Sometimes, the spelling of a word stumps me. Writing apps often use spell-checker to correct typos. Other times, I want to be sure the word has the correct meaning. Spell-checker can give me odd choices of replacement words. There are times I seem to use the same word several times in the same paragraph. That is when I turn to the thesaurus for help. It ~~helps~~ assists me to find other words with similar meanings.

Another option is to talk to someone. Conversations allow you to use the dialogue to bounce ideas around. This is a technique that we use frequently in the Alternative Book Club. As we write our chapters, we share them with each other to get feedback with the intent of clarifying our content. These are constructive discussions that help elevate our abilities as we take the time to be intellectual writers.

These discussions lead me to another aspect of finding the right words.

How to Explain What You Do Not Understand Yourself

As a parent, there have been times when my son would come up with a question that I struggled to answer. Often, they were about why other people were behaving the way they were. I was usually able to convince him as a grade-schooler that they may have been having a bad day. "Why?" While I could make up an imaginary scenario, I did not usually know the real reason.

When his questions progressed to how things are engineered, I learned to take a different approach when I did not know the exact details he sought. Those times became opportunities to admit that we would need to do some research to find the answers. The same is true with writing. There are times that I need to research the topic to gain clarity and become a bit scholarly.

What is my takeaway from this approach? My son, now in his thirties, is a test engineer! He is not afraid to learn what it takes to get answers to his questions. He has developed a love of testing the limits of the machinery he watches come down the assembly line. Custom parts to solve problems are researched and developed. I find research to be a key element that got him where he is. Research leads to learning and creates knowledge and understanding.

Writing at a Level Your Reader Can Comprehend

The challenge of research is how to convey your findings in a way that the reader can comprehend. As noted above, when my son was young, I had to handle explanations at a level that he could grasp. As he grew, the explanations became more technical. We literally would talk through every step of how something was done.

For example, when he was in Cub Scouts, this Den Mother was teaching the den how to tie various knots. Working with ropes as we moved through the motions was one thing. The real discussion became about where and when each type of knot would be used. Square knots and half-hitches were easy for them to understand. The next meeting brought them a different knot that they were unsure about, especially when they found a collection of neckties replacing the ropes. The five boys in that den spent an hour learning how to tie a full Windsor knot to make those neckties hang handsomely around their necks. Those ten-year-olds had fun showing their new skill to their parents that day. The dads were heard saying that was a skill they did not learn until high school. Those boys were able to comprehend the instructions. Why wait until high school?

My point is that you have to know your audience. Younger people may need simple instructions with clear steps. Those high school boys may just mess with the tie on their own and figure it out, watch a video, or, just get an older man to tie it for them. (My husband used clip-ons until he managed to figure it out.)

As an adult now, my son is a test engineer. He had to test the seals on a dishwasher. While it could be done just by watching as water was pumped through the unit, he needed to create an automated test. Rather than just telling me he created an automated test that not only checks water leaks, he told me the technical steps it takes to certify the seals, pumps, and electrical systems. While a ten-year-old would be satisfied to know that machinery tests other machinery, I am sure my son could write quite an intellectual paper that would impress Dr. Wolff.

Have you noticed how few words are in books for young readers? They have a limited vocabulary. As their vocabulary grows, their comprehension grows. Let me share a bit of research on the average difference between the vocabulary of school-aged children.

According to theschoolrun.com, a five-year-old has an average vocabulary of 2,000 to 2,100 words. A twelve-year-old has an average of 50,000 words according to this site, and "Six-year-olds have 2,600 words in their expressive vocabulary (words they can use) while they have 20,000-24,000 words in their receptive vocabulary (words they understand.)" Isn't that interesting?

6 years	2,600 words expressive vocabulary (words they can use) 20,000-24,000 words receptive vocabulary (words they understand)

While an adult should have a much larger vocabulary, if you are not versed in the topic you are writing about, using scholarly words rather than intellectual words is likely to result in your reader not comprehending your writing. My point is to save your scholarly words for a scholarly audience. Use those techy words with your techy audience. Avoid an abundance of jargon otherwise. Write to the intelligence level of your reader.

When you do not know your audience, stay away from challenging words. Remember, word choices matter.

Use of Filler Words

Another vocabulary issue that we need to address is the use of filler words. When speaking, people often use ahs and ums to fill the air while they come up with their next words. When writing, I see frequent use of "so," "and," or even "I." These are referred to as crutch words. They are words that we lean on when we do not know what else to say. If you are writing a high school paper with a goal of a certain number of words, they count.

However, they do not show intelligence. As Dr. Wolff suggests in the introduction to this chapter, removing unnecessary words will improve how intelligent you sound. I encourage you to reread those initial thoughts you wrote to eliminate any verbosity.

Does each word contribute to making your point? Are you using fluffy adjectives to describe that oozing, bubbly, seeping, warm, wet water leak when oozing warm water leak is sufficient?

Are you using "and" to tie together run-on sentences? "So, the water was leaking and, so, he was going to have to find the source." Break that into two sentences. "The water was leaking. He needed to find the source." This will allow the reader to mentally pause to absorb what is happening. How? The period is like a stop sign on the road. While some people only slow down, letting your tires come to a complete stop allows you to regroup before driving ahead. Regrouping allows your brain to process the information that you just received. I consider "so" to be the equivalent of potholes in the reading or listening road. Please eliminate them!

Word choices matter.

Use of Repetitive Words

I mentioned this earlier when ~~I listed some~~ citing tools I use when writing.

Let's use the next two sentences as an example. "A thesaurus can be helpful when you use words like 'helpful' twice in one sentence. Your word choice is even less helpful when the same word is used several times in a paragraph meant to be helpful."

Here are some alternative words my thesaurus suggests for helpful: advantageous, benefic, beneficent, beneficial, benignant, favorable, friendly, good, kindly, profitable, and salutary.

With these options, let's try a rewrite. "A thesaurus can be advantageous when you use words like "helpful" twice in one sentence. Your word choice is even less favorable when the same word is used several times in a paragraph meant to be beneficial."

Small changes in word choices can have an impact.

<u>Conclusion</u>

Did you notice the strike-throughs as you read this chapter? While we tend to edit those out of our finished work, these are here to help you see exactly how my writing continues to be revised. Why? I want to come across as intelligent rather than scholarly. Dr. Wolff makes the point with his quote. I want to address my reader at an appropriate level of comprehension to increase their understanding of the presented material. I do not want to take all day to say what needs to be said succinctly. Verbosity may fill pages…while less verbiage makes the point.

Choose your words wisely!

Reflection Questions

1. List your favorite crutch words.

2. Identify which ones just fill space.

3. Look up words that you repeat in a thesaurus. Make a list of alternative words. Develop a practice of looking up more words in the future as you identify them.

4. Write a short story for a five-year-old.

5. Rewrite that story for a teenager.

6. Write a version of the story for an intellectual adult.

Story Telling vs Story Writing

By: Janel Asche

"Of course, a good story is a good story. One art form is not better than the other. Oral storytelling can enhance writing and writing can enhance oral storytelling--I often write about the stories I tell, in order to understand them."

~ Priscilla Howe, Storyteller

Storytelling has a very long history. How long? How do we know? For one thing, Homo sapiens, modern humans, populated parts of the planet possibly as far back as 300,000 years ago. Obviously, someone figured out how to communicate. Man is, after all, a social creature.

Even long, long ago, there must have been family groups of at least mothers and children as human children are not biologically precocious. We don't stand up within moments of our birth or run within our first few hours of life. We are fully dependent on our parents, especially our mothers, for food and protection. Therefore, it is highly unlikely we went hundreds of thousands of years without communicating.

Our predecessors must have used drawings in the dirt and on cave walls to communicate. They must have created hand signs and used body language for a good while. Finally, words were developed to tell the stories of the hunt or where to find fruits, vegetables, and herbs. They had to describe how all those foods could be prepared and which could be used to heal. They had to tell stories about the dangers around them, maybe about a family member who died from eating poisonous mushrooms or about a wild cat prowling, looking for prey. Clearly, stories were being told. However, the earliest known written language dates back only to 3200 BCE. That means for approximately 99% of Homo sapiens' existence our storytelling was principally oral.

Many cultures revolved around oral tradition passing down the history of their people story by story. Some of those stories might be hours long yet meticulously memorized and related generation after generation through centuries. Few among us outside of that culture would sit still for an hours-long recitation. We will, though, spend hours reading written stories. How do modern oral storytelling and written storytelling differ?

How You Came to the Story

Perhaps the very first difference between a written and oral story is how you came to experience it. Was it attention-grabbing cover art, work-required convention attendance, or library story hour? Perhaps it was a book club selection, a college valedictory address, or a church sermon. A vast variety of stories surrounds us. Making a choice can be difficult.

When searching for a story, oral or written, you might seek out recommendations to guide you. Otherwise, for a written work, the first thing that draws you to a new book is probably the cover. Engaging artistry will make a reader pick up the book. A tantalizing title comes next. Is it straightforward like "The Story of My Life," by Helen Keller? Perhaps it's more thought-provoking like "Lord of the Flies," by William Goldberg, or "All the Light We Cannot See," by Anthony Doerr. Maybe the title belies the power of the story. Who would pick up George Orwell's book "Animal Farm" expecting the compelling political satire inside the simple cover? Perhaps you would do so after reading publicized reviews or maybe the blurb and reviews on the cover. All of the above can help you decide if the story will be a good one.

Finding oral stories can be both difficult and easy, depending on your perspective. It can be more difficult to find professionally presented oral stories. You cannot just walk into a store and find one. Finding formal oral stories requires a more deliberate approach. You can use a search engine to find one-man or one-woman shows on Broadway or in community theaters. For example, "The Search for Signs of Intelligent Life in the Universe," originally performed by Lily Tomlin or John Leguizamo's "Freak." You can similarly seek storytellers like Priscilla Howe. Many comedians and ministers are excellent raconteurs, as well. Formally presented oral stories by non-professionals often come to us as surprises. In today's world, an outstanding commencement address may go viral, bouncing around the internet for weeks, months, or even years.

On the other hand, informal, amateur oral stories fill our world. Every one of us knows someone—a family member, friend, or coworker—who tells amazing stories. It could be a masterful joke or a fascinating family history. As the quote above notes, "A good story is a good story." The great number of social media outlets provides virtually anyone a platform for sharing tales that reach around the world, generating laughter and touching hearts everywhere.

Oral Stories Are Time-bound

Another difference between written stories and oral ones is that storytelling speeches are normally bound by time limitations for the event. Most presentations given at public speaking clubs are five to seven minutes long. Commencement addresses generally run five to ten minutes long, though in some cases, they continue for up to twenty minutes. Keynote addresses run from thirty to sixty minutes long. In all cases, though, the event organizers will have defined your time slot. With limited time, it is important to make your points succinctly. To meet the time limits, you may find yourself whittling away words or even syllables in your presentation.

Equally important, points must be made memorably. With the written word, if a character pops up again after being introduced chapters ago, the reader can always leaf back to the proper page for a quick who's who reminder. Not so in speeches. Once the words are heard, your audience has to remember them or be specifically reminded later. There is no "look-back" option with a speech. For that reason, a speaker may rely heavily on archetypes or even stereotypes to lock a character into the listener's memory.

Another factor in time limitation for oral storytelling is the attention limit of the audience. That can vary with the age of your listeners and the subject matter at hand. Six-year-olds may be all ears for even a keynote-length speech about their favorite dinosaurs, but might not last even thirty seconds in a lecture on nuclear medicine. Similarly, a thirty-year-old may not last through more than one round of animal introductions on Old MacDonald's farm.

Written Stories Are Time Indeterminate

A very significant difference between the two art forms is that written works have no set length. Given, books for children do have word count limits for picture books, first readers, chapter books, and young adult novels. However, with books for adults, limits are more open-ended. Picture books and first readers are designed to be finished in one sitting. Other categories may be read over days or weeks. With that degree of freedom, it's much easier to include many characters, multiple settings in time and space, and much more detailed development of characters. Readers can immerse themselves in the author-invented world rather than briefly visit that created by an oral storyteller.

Performative Versus Static

Much like a play, oral stories change with every telling. Even reciting the very same words with identical intonations and inflections, the story will not be exactly the same every time. Much of the difference has to do with audience response. That can change the energy and body language of the performers or even change the length of the presentation. As a performative work, when it's over, it's over. It may create a lasting impression, but, unless it's recorded, there's no way to recapture that exact storytelling experience.

Conversely, written works are static. Once they are written, they are there for the reader to consume as many times as they like, each time the same, verbatim. Although a reader may take away different points with each reading, (new lessons or new insight), the words remain the same. That means the author needs to invest much time and many rounds of editing to build enough detail to represent the body language, intonation, and inflections readily made clear in the oral telling.

In some cases, you might be able to fix an image into the mind of the reader with very few words. Something as simple as "his brow raised in suspicion" may be enough. We all understand what that looks and even feels like. However, something more complex like a fight scene can become extremely laborious where the author walks a thin line between clear depiction and losing the reader in over-description. Think of the days, weeks, and even months spent defining and choreographing sword battles in movies. Accomplishing the task in a written tale can become tedious for both the writer and the reader.

Character Development Approach

Speakers and authors have many tools to make their characters more real. Archetypes are one tool for character creation. According to psychologist Carl Jung, there are twelve archetypes universally understood. His list includes the Innocent, the Everyman, the Hero, the Outlaw, the Explorer, the Creator, the Ruler, the Magician, the Lover, the Caregiver, the Jester, and the Sage. Merely reading through the list most likely triggered your mind to fantasize such characters. We are, according to Jung, hard-wired to identify them. However, it is unlikely that the writer would point blank define a character in their story by one of the archetype designations. Instead, where the character fits in that list would be made clear via more subtle means through actions, words, and attitudes. Archetypes require actual character development.

In contrast, stereotypes can be summed up in a very short description. They are especially convenient for speeches where time is at a premium. As a speaker, you can use them to quickly insert a minor character's persona into the listener's imagination. Stereotypes like "dare-devil skateboarder" or "self-absorbed diva" bring very clear images immediately to mind. You have a good idea about what they wear. You know how they walk, talk, and interact with others. In your mind's eye, you can even envision your characters' friends and imagine their favorite foods, hangouts, and activities. Not everyone will hold the same t images. One listener may imagine a young man wearing just street clothes and a headband, his wild red hair streaming behind him as he shreds the half-pipe. Another might think of a young woman with tattoos and a buzz cut as she grinds down a stair railing sporting a full set of pads along with a secured helmet. Safety, after all, is important, even for daredevils. Although there's not enough information conveyed for a definitive, universal image, each member of the audience has conjured a specific character from just a few well-chosen syllables.

Written works spend more time developing a cast of characters. The story may include every one of Jung's archetypes or only a few. In a story like J.R.R. Tolkien's "The Hobbit" or "The Lord of the Rings," it's easy to spot the majority of the types. However, many works incorporate just a small subset.

Plot and Conflict

Two elements that every good story needs are plot and conflict. Time-limited oral narratives, though, are more restricted in plot complexity and number of significant conflicts. In a written story, numerous sub-plots help maintain reader interest over hundreds of pages, but too many sub-plots in an oratory can be confusing. As for the second element, while every story will have a principal conflict, there are often multiple conflicts throughout the tale. There may be an overarching conflict of man vs nature, but there may be critical conflicts of man vs man or man vs himself at work, as well. Understandably, an extensive written work will comprise many more conflicts than an oral recitation.

A Case in Point

What follows is an example of a speech and related short story. Note the differences. Notice the level of detail in each, the extent of the description of the scene, and the necessary devotion to describing actions and movements that a speaker could easily depict physically. The speech leaves little room for background information. Nor does it accommodate extra characters. How does that affect your interpretation of the stories?

Volunteers

"I love volunteers. I love those individuals and groups jumping in to make a difference. They show up to make life better, easier, and happier. I especially love those volunteers I meet in the spring and summer as I work in my gardens. This year, there were many. Whether they're there because of faulty fall clean-up or due to canine affinity for juicy red orbs, I am fairly surrounded by volunteers.

Yes, this year we have more volunteer tomato plants than plants we purchased. What's more, each of the freebies is well ahead in maturity, even though they did not peek through the ground until after the larger, store-bought ones had been put in the soil. All told, we have four bonus babies—one rising up in the middle of the yard, thriving where the grass is a brown scuff no longer growing enough to need cutting. I will not kill a volunteer. When one enters my life, I just let the joy sink in. Our favorite volunteer, though, was Wandering Walt.

A few years ago, at the start of the summer, I was pulling weeds from the cracks of our four-slab concrete patio when I happened upon a leaf that looked like no weed I knew. It did, though, look familiar. I just could not quite place what it was...so I left it. As the days passed, I became more convinced of its identity. I'm not really sure how it came about. Perhaps a seed-spitting contest was responsible, or maybe my young daughter spilled a seed or two from the pack she brought out to the garden plot, but I had a lovely young watermelon plant sprouting from the dead center of my patio.

You can imagine everyone's surprise. It was a miracle on the order of a virgin birth! We discussed what to do. Surely, we should accept this miracle. After all, the seeds we planted with the vegetables were carried away by a swarm of ants. We listed the pros and cons. Yes, it would cover part of the patio, but there would be very minimal weeding. Cement makes excellent mulch. The thought of having freebie melons in a few months settled the issue. Week by week the winding watermelon vine wandered across the patio, wending its way among planters and under the weathered wood steps. As the vine grew on us, we decided it should have a name. So it was that he became Walter, the Wandering Watermelon. Occasionally, we shifted Walt's vines to keep a clear walking path for our dogs and ourselves. We watched his yellow blooms emerge and witnessed the bees pollinating them. Then, we watched the closed flowers become bulbous baby melons.

Dreaming of a healthy harvest, we made bets on just how many melons would reach our picnic table. The early answer was, "Surely eight!" As they swelled to six inches, however, a certain large-mouthed dog decided a couple were his new toys. He pulled them off the vine and brought them to us, wanting to play fetch. The remaining melons continued to grow and grow. The sad thing about growing watermelons is that it tests your patience. When you think that a melon has definitely grown large enough, you decide to pick it, cut it open, and find that it is barely beyond white inside, with far more rind than flesh. We lost two more that way. I swear I heard Walt's wicked, twisted laughter mocking our mistake. In the end, we did get to eat three very tasty free melons and gave a fourth to a neighbor.

I hate to show favorites, but Walter ranks number one among our memorable volunteers. Walter is also the reason for the high survival rate of our local volunteers. Thanks to him, I relish every single one. Tom, Tammy, Roma, and Cherry Tomato have Walter to thank, as do the four corn brothers and that unknown squash among the beets. They all are bearing the joy of surprise to our summer, along with all the tasty goodness that will grace our table because of them. My humble advice to you is— value your volunteers."

Speech Characteristics

The speech provides a brief tale, but there's no backstory. There are none of the details that put me in the mindset that volunteers were not just weeds. They served a vital purpose even when a bit annoying and inconvenient. What made me value those volunteers? Here's a short story that makes those points clear.

Volunteer

Rip. Rip. Rip. Rrrip. "That was a monster!" Why did I sign up for this? Why, indeed? Why would anyone volunteer to weed? Did you ever notice it's a four-letter word? Let me tell you. There were a lot more four-letter words running through my head, searching for a way out. I threw up a few more mental blocks to keep them safely confined. Ironically, those words were not all made of a mere four letters each. Why would I subject myself to the mind-numbing, finger-cramping, downright dirty business of weeding? Privacy—not the all-alone type of privacy, but the kind shared.

It was one of the few times I could spend hours alone with my mom. With six kids in the house, it was next to impossible to get one-on-one time with either of our parents. Mom, though, was an avid gardener with sprawling beds of flowers on three sides of our home. A thick, solid line of irises on the far side of the driveway made up for the barren fourth, windowless side of the house. That side faced the highway. Not one of my siblings wanted anything to do with gardening. I saw my opportunity and jumped at it. I became Vice President of Garden Maintenance. That meant…weeding, lots and lots of weeding. To reach the illustrious title of V.P.G.M. required some serious training.

"Which ones are weeds?" I asked, kneeling in the dew-soaked grass as we tackled the southern strip of landscaping.

"Everything that doesn't look like this," Mom replied, indicating her prized peony bushes. Their large dark green leaves would form a dense background for heavy blooms of white, pink, and deep fuchsia. The weight of those giant flowers would cause their stems to arch toward the ground, stopping scant inches above the grass. Their heady fragrance would fill the air, smelling more like roses than roses do themselves. At the moment, though, only small buds tipped the branches.

I looked carefully around and yanked everything that looked out of place, including every blade of grass encroaching on the flower bed. I learned some names along the way. Wood sorrel was the four-leaf clover look-alike with leaflets that sometimes became folded hearts. It was so cute with its bright yellow, five-lobed flowers. I called them star-hearts and hated to pull them, but they were weeds. According to Mom, they had to go. The spurge had to go, too. That was one weed I was happy to be rid of. It always reminded me of the Black Cat firecrackers my brother would set off. They sounded too much like machine gun fire to me. Spurge was like a tangled web of those long strings of explosive bits stretching across the ground. It made me cringe. I would rip it out and violently shake it off as if it would blow off my hand. Then there was foxtail. The rest of us, including my dad, called it tickle-weed, with good reason. Given my druthers, I would have let them grow so I could torment my little sister with them. She hated being tickled.

The peony bed was pretty easy to weed from the "what's-it" standpoint. Some of the other beds were more challenging. Spotting the weeds in the tall phlox that I loved was more challenging. However, by that time, I knew a foxtail on sight and discovered I could slip a few misses of it in the phlox to feed my tickle-weed need. The mums were the worst. One weed, which shall remain nameless, because I had yet to identify it, looked far too much like the mums themselves. Were I to name it, I would call it "the deceiver." It was very successful at hiding its true identity. Though it did not appear hazardous, its stealthy behavior made me very suspicious. That is exactly what I told Mom.

"You're anthropomorphizing and looking at it teleologically," she said.

"What?"

"You're ascribing human characteristics to a non-human entity. The weed is not deliberately hiding. It has no decision-making ability. Hiding is not a goal. Decades or centuries of mutations have made it look more and more like a plant we consider desirable. Because it looks so

174

much like something that would not be killed, it and its daughters survive while others of its kind are destroyed.

"It's the same with viceroy butterflies. You know. The ones that look like monarchs but do not have the milkweed poison built up in them. Birds and other predators avoid them because, over the decades or centuries, mutations have caused the viceroys to look more and more like the butterflies that make them sick. Viceroys live, because animals have learned monarchs make them sick."

"How do the animals know?"

"Through experience or possibly even through teaching. One nasty taste might be enough for them to avoid monarchs in the future. Even animals learn from their mistakes. Sometimes they learn faster than a lot of people I know." She nudged me with her elbow and flashed a mischievous grin.

I knew what she was thinking—shoes. I ducked my head sheepishly. For years she had begged me to take care of my shoes. They sprouted up everywhere they shouldn't be, like weeds. Exasperated, she once pulled all those weeds by ones and twos, bagged them up, and hid them.

It took me a long time to figure out what happened to them. Yet today, there's a pair of my shoes in virtually every room in the house. Yes. With certainty, there are a few animals that learn faster than I do.

Although she teased me about shoes and other things as we weeded, those hours ripping out green interlopers also led to a lot of storytelling. I heard tales of my mother's childhood no other sibling did. The stories that most fascinated me were about growing up in the Great Depression. She would talk about eating eggs and potatoes for breakfast, potatoes and eggs for supper, and mustard sandwiches for lunch. It was a balanced diet, after all. If you imagine the mustard sandwiches as the fulcrum, the other meals are perfectly balanced.

Back in the Great Depression, you had to do whatever it took to "make do." That meant working hard, very hard, even for those many who were unemployed. Mom's family grew their food in a huge garden and canned every bit they could not eat right away. They also raised chickens for all those egg-based meals. Once a year, they killed some of the chickens. When they were very young, Mom and Aunt Ella hid in the bushes to escape the headless birds running seemingly straight at them. Finally, the chickens flopped to the ground, lifeless.

176

Then, it was plucking time. Fluffy bits of down drifted through the warm summer air as the women carefully pulled off all of the birds' feathers to be saved for making pillows. Finally, they cooked and canned the meat, in a much-used pressure cooker.

Later, my grandmother opened a jar of chicken, along with some garden peas and carrots she had canned. Next, she mixed up a simple dough of flour, milk, and egg and rolled it out to stretch across the counter. A cutting wheel left tumbles of fresh noodles in its wake. Then, the doughy strands were dropped into steaming broth one at a time so they would not stick together. Each noodle was welcomed to the pot by a crowd of bubbles boiling up around it, instantly transforming it to a pale, semi-rigid ribbon. The result of all that labor, from garden to plucking, to canning and cooking, was a delicious chicken noodle soup like no other. Yes. They worked very hard in the Depression, but it ensured they would have food throughout the winter.

Listening to my mother's tales made weeding go faster, or at least more pleasantly.

When I had acquired sufficient V.P.G.M. skills, I was promoted to work in the vegetable garden. By work, of course, I mean weeding. The timing was just right. A couple of weeks ago, I helped Mom plant the seeds and starts in neat, straight rows, all measured carefully for depth, distance, and spacing. I helped with building the mounds for planting the squash and cucumbers, too. Weeding would be a breeze. Everything we wanted to keep should be in those neat rows and tidy mounds. Everything else, I knew now, was a weed. I got to work. Rip, rip, rrrrip, ri—.

"Stop! Not that one!" my mom cried.

"Why not? It's a weed, right? It's not in a row or mound we planted. It doesn't even look like anything else here."

"But does it look like a weed you know?"

"Um…not really."

"That's because it's not a weed. It's a volunteer."

"What's that supposed to mean?" The only volunteers I knew of then were those for the March of Dimes like Mom and those crazy enough to volunteer to help weed, like me.

"That, my dear, is a watermelon. I don't often plant them, because they take up a lot of space. However, we could

178

spend dozens of dollars buying fully-grown fruit, or take advantage of this lucky surprise. We did not even have to buy and plant seeds for it. No cost, all gain. We'll leave it. It's in a good spot to minimize interference with the other plants. We can shift the vines if we need to. Let's leave it." So, we did.

In the coming weeks, Mom's stories included many about volunteers she had tended over her decades of gardening. Once they had a whole row's worth of corn plants scattered haphazardly throughout the garden. Another time, it was a bushy bank of tomatoes along the hedge. A repeated surprise was the okra. Even though she planted it exactly one time in her entire life, it showed up seven years in her garden, each time providing enough for at least one or two meals. In the Depression, every bit of food counted, every bit.

"Always appreciate volunteers," Mom said.

This spring, I thought back to those early lessons in gardening. As I was weeding between the four cement slabs of our patio, I came across a single leaf that did not look like any weed I knew. It was, though, very familiar. Just like in that garden long ago, a watermelon sprouted, through unknown means. Another volunteer was born.

In appreciation, we let it grow.

Short Story Characteristics

In contrast to the speech, the short story tells a more detailed account that explains the birth of my affinity for volunteers. There is more descriptive language to create the setting for each scene—dew-soaked grass, heady fragrance, and bushy banks. Through dialog and interaction, the characters' traits are revealed—curiosity, resilience, and perseverance. There is history and a backstory with tales from each character's past.

Conclusion

Clearly, there are significant differences between storytelling and story writing. Many of the differences are based on the time limitations for oral storytelling events. Written works allow readers to consume the story on their own terms, reading all in one sitting or across days, weeks, or months. Written works also allow and, often, necessitate the writer to incorporate much more descriptive language than in oral telling.

The performative nature of storytelling relies on the teller's body language, intonations, and inflections, whereas story writing must rely on words alone to try to communicate all of those aspects. As a performance, each storytelling is unique, even when the story is the same, while written works are static—

unchanging. Only the reader changes, not the words. Plot, conflict, and character development are also affected by the time restrictions on oral storytelling.

Story writing accommodates much more detail and complexity than storytelling. In the end, though, as Priscilla Howe points out, "a good story is a good story. One art form is not better than the other," and each form can enhance the other.

<u>Reflection Questions</u>

1. Read the chapter on Point of View, if you have not already done so. How effective was the first-person perspective in these stories? Why did I choose first-person over the more common third-person perspective?

2. How would telling this story in third-person affect the feel of it?

3. How does the written story enhance the oral story?

4. How were non-verbal cues communicated in written form? Were they successfully made clear? Granted, you have not had the opportunity to view the speech, but can you imagine the body language in both the oral and written forms of the story?

5. Do you have a favorite short story? Try to compose an oral story that both represents and builds upon the written tale.

Finding Your Stories

By: Mark Fegan

"Tell them (what you'll tell them), tell them, tell them (what you told them)."

~ Anon

"Tell a story, make a point. Tell a story, make a point. Tell a story, make a point."

~ Anon

"We hold these truths to be self-evident..."

~ T. Jefferson

"Anything that can go wrong will go wrong and at the worst possible time."

~ E. A. Murphy Jr.

"Murphy was an optimist!"

~ O'Toole

*"quod erat demonstrandum ("**that which was to be demonstrated**")"*

~ Any Geometry student

This book is a collection of essays discussing various aspects of stories; finding stories, writing stories, and telling stories to name a few. In this chapter, I will discuss various techniques for finding stories that you can use to add interest to your presentation. You may notice some repetition from time to time; this is intentional as I first develop one or two stories, and then illustrate how I used the stories in developing larger presentations. The stories I will present were developed as parts of spoken presentations. (For more information on developing stories for oral presentations, see Randy Prier's chapter "Stories for Speakers.)

Consider this common scenario: you have been asked to prepare and present information on a topic of interest to your organization. This may be job-related or as part of a program for a church or other community organization.

The Triple-T

Once you decide on the topic for your presentation, you will need to build your presentation. One structure that is commonly used for presentations such as this is what I call the *Triple-T*. The *Triple-T*, which has been described by numerous education specialists, consists of three parts: an introduction, the body of the presentation, and the conclusion. Briefly, the parts are

1. Introduction: Tell them (what you plan to tell them)
2. Body: Tell them
3. Conclusion: Tell them (what you told them)

Triple-T is a framework that can be used in a variety of situations such as presenting information to a group as part of your job or teaching a class. It can also be used to provide the structure for an article such as this one.

The Introduction: Tell them (what you plan to tell them)

The introduction is your opportunity, as a presenter, to tell your audience what to expect from your presentation. You should briefly identify the points you are planning to discuss in your presentation. Although very brief, it should clearly identify the topics you plan to discuss in the presentation.

The Body: Tell them

The body of the presentation contains the meat; the information you want your audience to understand. You present the information to your audience. There are several ways you can organize and present this information, but one commonly used pattern can be summarized this way:

```
repeat (until done) {
    tell a "story"
    make a "point"
}
```

Please note that the story need not be fictional; rather it is a narrative that supports the point. Depending on the presenter and the intended audience the "story" may be an anecdote, a personal story, a quick example, or any narrative that illustrates the point you are making.

Also note that although I have described the contents of the body of the presentation as a series of "tell a story, make a point" couplets, in practice I find myself reversing the process. I find it easier to develop the content by deciding on one or more points and then finding a story to emphasize each point.

Conclusion: Tell Them (what you told them)

Like the introduction, the conclusion should be brief. In your conclusion, you simply summarize the topics you have covered in the presentation. This will serve as a quick reminder of the purpose of your presentation.

Putting it all together

Now that we have covered the basics of designing a presentation, it's time to shift our focus to finding stories and incorporating those stories into larger presentations. We will look at two types of stories: personal stories and stories drawn from the world in general. Both types of stories will enhance a presentation.

Finding a Personal Story

One of the most powerful ways to illustrate a point is to tell a personal story. We all have memories we can recall and develop into personal stories. How do you create a good personal story? Note: Several years ago, the Alternative Book Club was looking for an alternative mode to reach our intended audience. One idea that we decided to pursue was to design and present a series of workshops on various aspects of writing and publishing books. I was the project lead for the effort. Although the project was placed on hold, I did complete one of the proposed modules, *Getting Started (as an Author)*. The objective of that module was to provide a way for a person to start writing by writing a story about themselves. What follows is based on that module.

The process for writing a (short) personal story can be summarized in four steps:

A. **Select an idea for your story:** Pick an event in life you would like to utilize as an example in your presentation.

B. **Flesh out your idea:** Answer a few questions about the event. These are the usual questions: Who, What, When, Where, Why, How, and what was the result. (More on these questions in a bit.)

C. **Write your story:** Use the answers from #2 to write a short story describing the event. Try to keep the narrative/description to an "appropriate" length. What is "appropriate" will depend on several factors including the type of presentation (oral or written) and length of the presentation. Note: in presentations at Toastmasters International meetings most oral presentations are relatively short, approximately 7 minutes. For these presentations, my stories are usually 100 - 200 words long.

D. **Share/Utilize your story:** Add this story to the presentation.

The event I used to illustrate this story-writing process made an impact on me as a young student. The impact was so powerful that, after more than 60 years, I can still picture the classroom where it occurred; I even remember the teacher's name!

Since this is a personal story, based on my memories of an actual event, I am answering these questions in first person voice.

A: Select an idea, from your life, for your story

Another boring day in Arithmetic class. I was trying to draw a circle.

B: Flesh out your idea

1. The Location: A fifth-grade math class in a small public school.

188

2. The Players: Your humble author—a rather bored fifth grader; his Arithmetic teacher—a young female, new to the school.

3. The Topic: Long Division, which I already knew how to perform.

4. The Action: I started doodling, the teacher noticed and asked me what I was doing. I told her, "I am trying to draw a circle." She then shows me how to do it.

5. The Result: I learned there was much more to Mathematics than Arithmetic.

C: Complete the story

Once you have the basic idea for the story, you can write it out. As you do so, flesh out the details as needed. Make the story personal.

Here's the completed story:

One Day in Arithmetic Class

There I was, sitting in my fifth-grade classroom. It was an Arithmetic class. The topic was, once again, long division. I already knew how to do long division, so I decided to spend my time on something more interesting. I started doodling. The teacher, a recent college graduate, noticed what I was doing. Rather than calling me out in front of the class, she walked over and quietly asked me

"What are you doing?" Somewhat concerned about what was to follow, I replied "I'm trying to draw a circle." Imagine my surprise when, rather than yelling at me, she replied "Let me show you how it's done." She quietly returned to her desk and returned with a compass. Just as quietly, she drew a circle using the compass and left it with me to practice. With those few words and actions, she, rather than punishing me, introduced me to the world of Mathematics outside of Arithmetic.

This version of the story is told using First-Person voice; that is the story is being told from the viewpoint of the main character. Another commonly used voice is Third-Person. In Third Person, the story is told by a narrator who is watching or observing the action. The voice you use will depend on who is acting in the story. (For a more complete discussion of the use of voices in storytelling, see Keith Jones' chapter "Point of View")

Here's the same story told in third person:

One day in Arithmetic Class

A young boy, slightly bored in Fifth-grade Arithmetic class, quit doing his homework and started doodling in his notebook. His teacher, a recent college graduate, noticed this and asked, "What are you doing?"

Somewhat concerned about what might follow, he answered "I'm trying to draw a circle." Much to his surprise, she answered, "Let me show you how it's done." and introduced him to the compass. With those few words, that teacher, rather than punishing him, had introduced the young man to the world of mathematics outside of Arithmetic.

That's the basic technique for turning a memory into a story.

As you can see, a story can have different versions with varying degrees of detail and different voices. The basic facts of the story (who, what, when, where, why, and how) are present in both versions of the story, which version to create and use will depend on how you are presenting your story to an audience. (More on using a story in a presentation in the next section.)

Adding a Personal Story to a Presentation

A basic idea behind creating and telling stories is to add impact to presentations. As a result, many speakers commonly use stories to add more depth and a more human side to presentations. Of course, they may not call them stories; rather they may call them illustrations, anecdotes, or parables. The key, of course, is not what you call them but what they add to your presentation.

With that in mind, let's look at a story I included in a presentation I wrote and presented several years ago.

When I first joined Toastmasters International®, my journey through communication started with the Competent Communication manual. In preparation for one of the projects in the manual, I decided to talk about the often misunderstood phrase from the American Declaration of Independence. Thomas Jefferson, the main author of that document, wrote

> *"We hold these truths to be self-evident, that all*
> *men are created equal, that they are endowed*
> *by their creator with certain inalienable rights,*
> *that among these are Life, Liberty, and the*
> *Pursuit of Happiness."*

I decided to address two misunderstandings about this quote. Firstly, many people seem to believe this statement is from the United States Constitution, and secondly that Jefferson wrote "… Life, Liberty, and Happiness" rather than "… Life, Liberty, and the Pursuit of Happiness."

With that thought in mind, I decided to include a personal anecdote/story to illustrate my understanding of "the pursuit of happiness".

As described previously, here's how I developed that story.

Since this is a personal story, based on my memories of an actual event, I decided to answer these questions in first person.

A: Select **an idea, from your life, for your story**

>As a young Cub Scout, I entered my first Pinewood Derby.

B: Flesh out your idea

1. The Location: various sites around Cass Lake, Minnesota, in the spring of 1961.
2. The Players: Your humble author who decided to build his own racer.
3. The Topic: Building and racing that car.
4. The Action: I built the car, played with the car, broke the car, "fixed" the car, and finally "raced" the car.
5. The Result: the pursuit is frequently more important than the actual result.

C: Complete the Story

Here's the story as I included it in that presentation.

The Little Racer That Didn't

Back when I was in second grade, I joined the Cub Scouts. As is the case today, a highlight of the Cub Scout

193

year was the Pine Wood Derby. You've all seen the Pine Wood Derby car; it starts as a block of wood, four wheels, and four nails used as axles. In those days, you also had two wooden cross pieces you glued into the block to hold the nails.

I went to work, drew up my plans, and started cutting. My car was sure to be the winner. It looked like a classic Indy racer with a narrow front end and the wheels standing out from the body. Add the paint and numbers and it was ready to go.

The morning of the race, disaster struck. The right front wheel fell off. Being rushed for time (and like most males, unwilling to ask for help) I fixed it myself and jumped into the car with my folks, brothers, and sister.

We drove to the derby site, and I waited my turn.

When my name was called, I carried my car up to the track and placed it on the track with two other boy's cars. The starter lifted the gate, and they were off...

Well, the other two cars were off – mine just sat there. I was probably devastated, I don't recall!

While analyzing this presentation, I realized that it contained a second personal story. This story related how I reacted to what should have been a devastating setback in my childhood. Here's a description of the parts that went into this story:

Once again, since this is another personal story, based on my memories from my childhood, I am answering these questions in first person.

A: Select an idea, from your life, for your story

How I was impacted by losing the Pinewood Derby.

B: Flesh out your idea

1. The Locations: Cass Lake, Minnesota, and Eagle, Wisconsin. Spring of 1961 through the early summer of 1965.
2. The Players: Your humble author reflecting on his life after the not-so-great race.
3. The Topic: My life after the not-so-great race.
4. Action: I continued in Cub Scouts, won the Space Derby, and earned the Arrow of Light.
5. The Result: You just need to "get over it"!

C: Complete the Story

Here's how I described the after-effects of participating in the not-so-great race.

I learned some valuable lessons that day.

First, you should never use a rubber band to hold the axle on a Pine Wood Derby car.

More importantly, I learned that it's all right to fail provided you make the effort to succeed.

No, I didn't quit Scouts that day. I "stayed with the program" and a couple of years later even won my Pack's "Space Derby".

At the end of my time as a Cub Scout, I was one of the first two members of the Pack to earn the Arrow of Light, at that time the highest achievement available to a Cub Scout.

Adding the stories to a presentation

To complete my presentation, I added an introduction to set up my story and a section to provide a transition between the two personal stories. At the end of the presentation, I issued a challenge to my listeners. This served to complete the presentation and, I hoped, to trigger a response from the audience.

The overall structure of the presentation?

> *Introduction*
>
> *Personal story 1: the not-so-great race*
>
> *Transition between stories*
>
> *Personal story 2: Lessons learned*
>
> *Conclusion*

Here is the completed presentation with the additional material identified.

Title:

Freedom to Try; Freedom to Fail

Introduction:

We're all familiar with those stirring words, written so long ago by Thomas Jefferson

> *"We hold these truths to be self-evident; that all men are created equal, that they are endowed by their creator with certain inalienable rights, that among these are Life, Liberty, and the Pursuit of Happiness..."*

Seems these days some people get confused about Jefferson's words, believing they're part of the United

States Constitution. To set the record straight; they're in the Declaration of Independence.

But I'm not here to talk about Patriotic confusion; rather it's that "Pursuit of Happiness" phrase that I find interesting.

Too often people leave off the "Pursuit of" portion, somehow believing they should be automatically happy. "No work, no problems, mon."

The personal story:

Back when I was in second grade, I joined the Cub Scouts. As is the case today, a highlight of the Cub Scout year was the Pine Wood Derby. You've all seen the Pine Wood Derby car; it starts as a block of wood, four wheels, and four nails used as axles. I those days, you also had two wooden cross pieces you glued into the block to hold the nails.

I went to work, drew up my plans and started cutting. My car was sure to be the winner. It looked like a classic Indy racer with a narrow front end and the wheels standing out from the body. Add the paint and numbers and it was ready to go.

The morning of the race, disaster struck. The right front wheel fell off. Being rushed for time (and like most males, unwilling to ask for directions) I fixed it myself and jumped into the car with my folks, brothers and sister.

We drove to the derby site, and I waited my turn.

When my name was called, I carried my car up to the track and placed it on the track with two other boy's cars. The starter lifted the gate, and they were off...

Well, the other two cars were off – mine just sat there. I was probably devastated, I don't recall!

The transition between stories:

Many people today would say my dad should have checked my car and, realizing my fix was faulty, helped me do it right or that I should have gotten my dad to fix it for me. but I learned some valuable lessons that day.

The lessons learned – personal story 2:

First, you should never use a rubber band to hold the axle on a Pine Wood Derby car.

More importantly, I learned that it's all right to fail provided you make the effort to succeed.

No, I didn't quit Scouts that day. I "stayed with the program" and a couple of years later even won my Pack's "Space Derby". In fact, by the time I graduated from Cub Scouts in 1965, I was one of the first two members of the Pack to earn the Arrow of Light, which was, at that time, the highest achievement available to a Cub Scout.

The conclusion – lessons learned:

As I said, I was probably devastated that day. I really don't remember. When I look back at that day, I remember the sun, the blue sky, my car sitting at the top of the racetrack... I simply laugh.

I've heard it said, "If you don't grow, you die", or, as the Swiss artist and philosopher Paul Klee put it "Becoming is superior to being." But I think Jefferson put it best when he penned "Life, Liberty, and the Pursuit of Happiness."

Make your life a pursuit of happiness and I think you'll find yourself enjoying both the pursuit and the result.

As you can see, the presentation included more than just the story about my attempt to become a Pinewood Derby champion. It included a second story that summarized some of my experiences in Cub Scouts. The two stories were set up with an introduction; the conclusion was designed to bring the listener back to my premise that in life it's the pursuit of happiness that counts and is, in fact, more important than the results.

The critical point in adding stories to presentations is when you look at the complete presentation, any story you use in your presentation must support the thesis of the presentation.

Adding a third-person story to the presentation

There will be times when you desire to illustrate your presentation by adding a story about a historical or legendary figure. This approach can add depth to your presentation but keep in mind that the story must support your thesis rather than simply making your presentation more interesting or simply filling time.

Rather than testing your memory as is the case with many personal stories, citing information about a public or historical person is likely to involve some research.

As an example, consider the popular "laws" that people like to cite to "explain" why things occur. One of the most popular of these is "Murphy's Law" which people like to cite when things go wrong. Murphy's law is commonly quoted:

"Anything that can go wrong will go wrong."

201

Some people add:

(at the worst possible moment!)

There are several rewritings, extensions, and commentaries on Murphy's Law. One of my favorites is O'Toole's commentary:

"Murphy was an optimist!"

At one time, I was looking for a good topic for a presentation when I chanced upon the idea of unexpected occurrences. And Murphy's Law. And O'Tool's Commentary on Murphy's Law. I realized that I knew all about Murphy's Law but didn't know anything about Murphy.

That's an opportunity to write a story to support a presentation.

A: Select an idea for the Story

> I need to know more about Murphy of Murphy's Law fame.

B: Flesh out your idea

These additional details were the result of extensive (internet-based) research.

1. The Location: Not important

2. The Players: Edward A. Murphy, O'Toole

3. The Topic: Who is this Murphy character?

4. The Details: Murphy was a West Point graduate (1940), an Army Air Corp pilot, and a test engineer.

5. The Result: Murphy actually was an optimist as he believed good engineering could eliminate errors.

C: Complete the Story

Here's the story as I included it in that presentation.

Who is this Murphy Character anyway?

Edward Aloysius Murphy, Jr. was a West Point graduate (1940) who was a pilot in the Second World War. After leaving the Air Force in 1952, Murphy worked on many experimental aero-space programs including the X-15, the SR-71, and Project Apollo.

While still in the Air Force, in 1949, Murphy was an engineer on the MX81 project – working on rocket sleds for endurance testing. After an instrumentation failure on a test run, he is said to have coined his famous law.

Although an ever-popular excuse, Murphy claimed his law was intended as a guiding principle in "defensive" system engineering. His idea was that as systems became more complex, you need to anticipate, and then provide ways to recover from failure.

203

The story about Aloysius Murphy is an example of a research-based story told in the Third-Person. To complete the story, I had to look up the life and history of Murphy.

Another approach I have used is to draw on my academic and professional experience as a source for background in a story. Since the story is written about a subject with which I am familiar, it is natural to fill in the details based on what I know about the subject. (Of course, depending on the topic, it is sometimes necessary to do some research to flesh out the details in the story.)

Here's a second story I crafted, from my background as a Mathematics teacher, to shed further light on Murphy's Law.

A: Select an idea for the Story

    I need to provide a simple example of computing the likelihood of failure.

B: Flesh out your idea

    This information was developed primarily from my experience in studying and teaching Statistics.

    1. The Location: Not important

2. The Players: the laws of probability

3. The Topic: Really, how likely is failure?

4. The Details: Basic probability theory. Fractional arithmetic. A small, simple system.

5. The Result: In the simple system, there is a 2 in 3 chance that something will fail on any given day.

C: Complete the Story

Here's the story as I included it in that presentation

Really, how likely is failure?

A little simple math can help us decide. First a few facts:

1. Any event has a probability of occurrence, call it p.

2. All probabilities are *proper* fractions, i.e. $0 \leq p \leq 1$.

3. If you multiply two proper fractions, the result is smaller than either of the original fractions.

4. When you combine events, you multiply their individual probabilities.

With these facts, and a bit of beginning Calculus, you can prove Murphy's Law. But, since time is short, let's consider an example instead.

Consider a system that contains 10 components, each of which has a 90% chance of **not** failing each day. To determine the probability of no component failing on any

205

given day, simply multiply together 10 factors of 90% -- or 0.90^{10}, which equals roughly 35%. That is, on any given day, there is a 2 in 3 chance that something will fail.

The final Presentation

While the story of Murphy and his law provided a key portion of my presentation, there was more to the presentation including a personal story as an introduction, a short lesson in probability theory as applied to systems failure, and my conclusion.

The actual presentation contained some additional stories. One was a personal story about a memorable family Christmas. (This story was the inspiration for the presentation's title.) In addition, the presentation included a quick discussion of early attempts to develop electronic computers and a quick description, rather dated as I write this chapter, to illustrate the current state of electronic computing devices. The final story in the presentation is a quick lesson in probability to help answer the key question

"Was Murphy an optimist?

Here's the complete presentation:

Title:

Holiday Remembrances

Introduction:

Most of us have a wealth of Holiday Memories. One of my favorites is about a Christmas tree.

A Christmas Memory – Personal Story 1 (First person):

Prior to moving to Bellevue, Nebraska, my wife was the owner/operator of a performing arts studio in Auburn, Nebraska. One year, one of her clients gave us a used Christmas tree. It was a grand old tree, about 7 feet tall and very full. We used the tree every Christmas until that fateful one...

There we were, gathered around the tree while our youngest son was "playing Santa". As he reached under the tree for the next present, the trunk broke and the top "toppled" ...

Introduction, part 2:

Have you ever had "one of those days"? You know, the ones where nothing seems to go right? If so, you've probably heard of "Murphy's Law."

As you may have guessed, "Holiday Remembrances" isn't really my topic for tonight. I guess we can chalk it up to Murphy, the Murphy who was credited with the "law"—you know the one:

207

"Anything that can go wrong will go wrong."
(http://en.wikipedia.org/wiki/Murphy%27s_law)

Who is Murphy – Researched Story 2 (Third person):

But have you ever stopped to consider "Who was this Murphy character?" or "How did he know?"

Edward Aloysius Murphy, Jr. was a West Point graduate (1940) who was a pilot in the Second World War. After leaving the Air Force in 1952, Murphy went and worked on many experimental aero-space programs including the X-15, the SR-71, and Project Apollo.

While still in the Air Force, in 1949, Murphy was an engineer on the MX81 project – working on rocket sleds for endurance testing. After an instrumentation failure on a test run, he is said to have coined his famous law.

Although an ever-popular excuse, Murphy claimed his law was intended as a guiding principle in "defensive" system engineering. His idea was that as systems became more complex, you need to anticipate failures, and then provide ways to recover from those failures. I might add that I work on complicated computer systems for a living, and I always keep Murphy in mind.

208

Additional history –Story 3 (third person):

With the modern world becoming ever more dependent on ever more complex systems for everything from banking to air travel, the shadow of Murphy's Law hangs over us all.

In fact, in the post-World War II era, there were several attempts to develop true electronic computers. Many of these attempts came up against a single problem. Prior to 1948, electronic computer memory depended on radio tubes and radio tubes had three problems:

1. They required a lot of power,
2. they gave off a lot of heat, and
3. they really didn't last very long.

One early pundit predicted that computers would never amount to much simply because the radio tubes would burn out so frequently you wouldn't be able to keep the contraption running.

A footnote:

As an aside, at the time I originally wrote and gave this presentation, I owned a Palm Pilot. My Palm Pilot had a 128 Mega Byte memory. To duplicate that memory with radio tubes would require over 3 billion tubes. Imagine putting them in a box and trying to carry them around!

209

The question:

So, was Murphy right?

Some basic probability theory – story 4 (third person):

A little simple math can help us decide. First a few facts:

1. Any event has a probability of occurrence, call it p.
2. All probabilities are *proper* fractions, i.e. $0 \leq p \leq 1$.
3. If you multiply two proper fractions, the result is smaller than either of the original fractions.
4. When you combine events, you multiply their individual probabilities.

With these facts, and a bit of beginning Calculus, you can prove Murphy's Law. But, since time is short, let's consider an example instead.

Consider a system that contains 10 components, each of which has a 90% chance of **not** failing each day. To determine the probability of no component failing on any given day, simply multiply together 10 factors of 90% -- or 0.90^{10}, which equals roughly 35%. That is, on any given day, there is a 2 in 3 chance that something will fail.

Conclusion:

In real life, of course, systems have tens of thousands of components... But, of course, the reliability of each component is much higher. Is it any wonder that even the best-designed systems fail from time to time? Perhaps it's more of a tribute to Murphy that many systems operate for years without failing. Looks like Murphy was right after all even if he was a bit of an optimist!

Oh yes, the real title of my talk tonight: "Murphy was an optimist". That was O'Toole's reaction to Murphy's Law.

Once again, this presentation contained more than just the biographical information I was able to obtain about the real Murphy.

<u>A few words in conclusion</u>

My objectives in writing this chapter were 1) to provide you with a framework for writing stories and 2) to provide you with examples of how to incorporate your stories into presentations. Note that your presentation can be either oral or written. The two example presentations I have included were both written as speeches to be presented in front of an audience. Both speeches lasted approximately 7 minutes. (Incidentally, this chapter is another example of incorporating stories into a presentation.)

211

Using this framework, you will be able to write your own stories to add both a personal touch and added depth to your presentations.

"quod erat demonstrandum"

Reflection Questions

1. Consider an event from your life that might make a good story. Use the outline presented in this chapter to construct your story.

    a. Write down the idea for the story:

    b. Flesh out your story idea:

        i. The location:

        ii. The players:

        iii. The Topic:

        iv. The Details:

        v. The Result

   c. Complete/write your story:

2. Consider a topic that interests you. Use the outline presented in this chapter to construct a story based on this topic.

   a. Write down the idea for the story:

   b. Flesh out your story idea:

      i. The location:

     ii. The players:

    iii. The Topic:

    iv. The Details:

     v. The Result

c. Complete/write your story:

3. Pick either story that you constructed in questions 1 and 2. Develop a short presentation Using the TRIPLE-T structure.

a. Write a short introduction. (Tell them what you'll tell them.)

b. Use your chosen story as the body. (Tell them.)

c. Write a short conclusion. (Tell them what you told them.)

Meet our Authors

Janel Asche

Janel Asche is a contributing author for three previous books in the Spotlight on the Art series. She made her writing debut in Spotlight on the Art of Gratitude, wrote again for Spotlight on the Art of Speaking, and most recently wrote for Spotlight on the Art of Confidence.

A long-time application systems analyst, she wrote a new story for her life, one with a plot more suited to her gifts. One that involves telling stories every day and helping children create their own life stories.

Ms. Asche has lived in Nebraska all her life and has been married more than two-thirds of that time. She has four grown children, one granddaughter, and two grandkids racing to be the second grandchild to arrive. One of the two has only a small head start. The author's greatest passion is planting seeds and watching them grow. Whether it's a watermelon seed in the patio or the seeds of kindness and curiosity in the mind of a child, witnessing those seeds sprout and flourish invigorates her.

Contact Janel at janel@alternativebookclub.com.

Mark Fegan

Mark Fegan is a 1975 graduate of Morningside College in Sioux City, Iowa. His primary area of study was Mathematics Education. After graduation Mr. Fegan began a teaching career that lasted twenty years. After starting his career as a Junior High teacher in Minnesota, he taught High School Mathematics and Computer Science in Nebraska and completed this phase of his life in 1996 as an Assistant Professor at Peru State College in Nebraska. Along the way, he took a one-year hiatus to work in the garment industry and an additional year off for graduate school. Mr. Fegan earned his Master of Science in Education from Kearney State College in Nebraska in 1979. In 1996, Mr. Fegan changed his focus from education to Software Developer for Raytheon.

Mr. Fegan joined Toastmasters International in October 2009 and earned Distinguished Toastmaster status in August 2014. Mr. Fegan continues to be active in Toastmasters where he has served as District Director, the highest elective district office, for Toastmasters District 24 in 2020 - 2021.

In line with his lifelong interest in education, Mr. Fegan has also led the Alternative Book Club's Writers Workshop project--a set of workshop modules to assist an aspiring writer become a published author. This work is ongoing.

Mr. Fegan lives with his wife Rebecca in Bellevue, Nebraska, and continues to take an interest in education and helping others achieve their goals.

Contact Mark at: Mark@alternativebookclub.com

Rebecca Fegan

Rebecca Fegan is insatiably curious; she is a bibliophile and incessant researcher. Having worked many jobs throughout her life, she has gotten experience in quite a few fields and finds it fascinating to see correlations. In addition to her Music Education degree, she also picked up a degree in Business administration and is a Financial Analyst focusing on Investments. She is also an Accredited Coach by the European Mentoring and Coaching Council as a Founding Member of the Conscious Coaching Academy.

She has used her coaching acumen with her 5 children, her 5 grandchildren, and the thousands of students she's taught in her nearly six-decade career.

Growing up in a musical family, she is drawn to culture--art, literature, music, religion, and history. As the owner and operator of the Fine Arts Academy, and a member of Primerica Financial Services, she is embarking on a third business, The Fegan Method of Learning where she helps people acquire the information and skills they need to fulfill their dreams and destinies. She and Mark Fegan have been happily married since 1977.

As a member of Toastmasters, she has served in several capacities: District Administration Manager 2024-2025, District Club Retention Chair 2020-2023, District Treasurer, Division Director, and Area Governor. She currently belongs to three clubs. She really loves to compete!

Contact Rebecca at rebecca@alternativebookclub.com

Angie Garfield

Born and raised in Omaha, Angie knows her Midwest values are the foundation of her success. Angie has had successful years in the corporate world with a background in customer service, marketing, and management. Angie worked for OPPD for 37 years, and her entire career was in the Customer Service Division.

Expertise - Angie's expertise has been sought after for consulting both employees and management personnel seeking ways to communicate effectually to reach team and individual goals. One of Angie's strongest skillsets is helping others to uncover their highest performance capabilities. She has had consistent success working with teams to identify and meet group objectives and goals.

Business Owner

Angie created Customer First Success Inc. Company Mission - *to assist clients in exceeding their customers' expectations through internal, effective, and efficient customer service processes.*

Angie has designed programs for all levels of company employees. The programs include:

- Communication Skills
- Team Building
- Team Environment Dynamics
- People Development
- Emotional Intelligence
- Goal achievement for individuals and teams
- Behaviors
- Resolving Conflict

Business Success

Angie facilitated her program 'Customer Service and Communication Basics' to hundreds of employees of all levels to various companies in Omaha. The companies include New Cassel Retirement Center, Metropolitan Utilities District (MUD), Omaha Public Power District (OPPD), and Complete Comfort Heating and Cooling.

Public Speaking

With over 30 years of public speaking experience, Angie is a current member of the National Speakers Association. She is also a past member of Toastmasters International. Her participation in Toastmasters included Area Governor of District 24 Toastmasters Omaha, Past Club President of local Toastmasters Club 455, past Toastmaster of the Year. Angie has presented to Senior Executives, International Professionals, and charitable organizations. She has also been a mentor/advisor to adult speakers.

Contact Angie at angie@alternativebookclub.com

Christine Jones

Christine Jones is a mother of two and grandmother of three. She has been married to Keith Jones for forty-five years. As a founding member, she has contributed to several of the Spotlight books. The process of writing for the books has been helpful in mastering new skills as she learns to tell stories. She has found that she enjoys sharing stories about her children with her grandchildren who usually laugh in disbelief that their parents were ever young.

Beyond those stories, she has not been one to use many words to express herself. She says what she means in only as many words as needed to get her point across. When she has a husband that likes to use many more words in a day than she does, it could be because she has trouble getting a word in edgewise. As an introvert, she is good with that set-up.

She knows that you will find this book helpful as you elevate your story-telling skills.

Contact Christine at Christine@AlternativeBookClub.com

Keith Jones

Keith Jones is the CEO, President and Founder of Kitewind LLC, a company formed to facilitate presentations, publishing, and consulting for individuals and corporations. He is a founding member of the Alternative Book Club.

During more than thirty years of being involved in the Toastmasters International organization, Keith refined his speaking skills resulting in several championships at the district level in Humorous, Tall Tales, and Evaluation contests. Keith has achieved the organizations highest designation of Distinguished Toastmaster (DTM). Keith has served as District Director for Toastmasters District 24 during the 2023-2023 year.

Keith has had the honor and privilege to be able to teach and instruct both youth and adults in the art of leadership. He has taught adults to successfully develop their leadership skills. Keith and his wife Christine are parents of two children and grandparents of three grandchildren. Keith is also a contributing author for eight other books published by the Alternative Book Club.

Contact Keith at Keith@alternativebookclub.com

Evelyn Mosley

Evelyn is a retired county mental health case manager. She enjoys writing about life events and how they can affect others as well as herself and responses to these events.

According to Evelyn, our memories are a great reference for these stories. She enjoys writing about people and emotional health.

She is the mother of two, grandmother of four, and great-grandmother of two. She resides in the Midwest with her husband, David.

Evelyn is also a member of the local chapter National League of American Pen Women, Inc., and The North Omaha Summer Arts Women Writers Group. Evelyn feels that writing is cathartic as well as healing.

Contact Evelyn at Evelyn@alternativebookclub.com

Randy Prier

Randy Prier is a 22-year veteran of the US Air Force, having retired as a Lieutenant Colonel in 1993. During his time in the Air Force, he served in a variety of positions from Student Squadron Commander to AF Liaison with the Government of the US Territory of Guam to Division Chief in Headquarters, Strategic Air Command. His postings ranged from the Republic of the Philippines and Guam to Offutt AFB, Nebraska, and Washington, D.C. Randy's military decorations include the Defense Meritorious Service Medal, the Meritorious Service Medal with three Oak Leaf Clusters, the Air Force Commendation Medal, and the Air Force Achievement Medal.

Randy graduated from the University of Nebraska with a B.A. in Political Science in 1968 and earned a Master of Arts degree in International Affairs from the Catholic University of America in 1982. As a member of Toastmasters International since 1981, Randy has earned the highest educational award of Distinguished Toastmaster three times and received the Toastmasters International Presidential Citation in 2006. He served as District Governor of Toastmasters District 24 (covering parts of Nebraska and Iowa) in 1992-3, earning the Distinguished District Award. From 2001-03, he served a two-year elected term on the Toastmasters International Board of Directors. As a frequent Toastmasters speech contest competitor, Randy has won District 24 championships in the International Speech, Humorous (twice), Evaluation and Table Topics contests. He has also been a runner-up in the District's Tall-Tale contest.

Randy and his wife, Kathy, have three grown children and five grandchildren. They live in Papillion, Nebraska, a suburb of Omaha.

Contact Randy at randy@alternativebookclub.com

More from the

Alternative Book Club

If you enjoyed this book, consider picking up a copy of our other books, *Spotlight on the Art of Grace, Spotlight on the Art of Resilience, Spotlight on the Art of Significance, Spotlight on the Art of Fear, Spotlight on the Art of Generating Energy, Spotlight on the Art of Gratitude, Spotlight on the Art of Speaking, and Spotlight on the Art of Confidence.*

In *Spotlight on the Art of Grace*, you will be moved by powerful stories of personal loss and triumph. You will learn how to mend fences, how to make the world better, and all the while do it with energy and with a smile.

"Each Chapter offers lessons in Grace, with the contributing author sharing relevant stories with insight and thought-provoking discussion questions. I am impressed with the depth and diversity of perspectives into Grace, as the compilations include resiliency, perseverance, forgiveness, constructive feedback, principles-based leadership, collaboration and valuing others. Well-done! A must-read for anyone in leadership, management, or any type of relationship and wants to keep it healthy!"
- **Sheryl Roush, Speaker, 17-time Published Author**

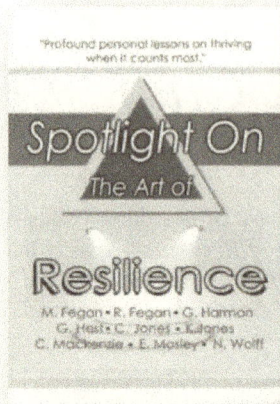

Spotlight on the Art of Resilience

The by powerful stories of resilience will be a source of hope in hard times These are stories of getting through the challenges that are thrown at you. These may be jobs, relationships, or health.

Written by most of the same authors who wrote the previous titles, we hope these books will prove to be as beneficial to you as it was for us to write them.

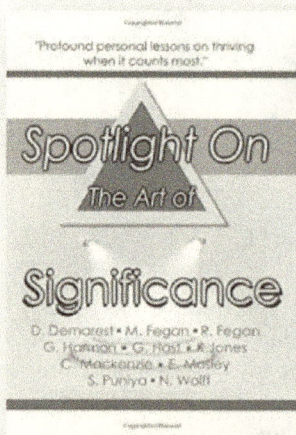

Spotlight on the Art of Significance

The stories in this book reveals the powerful impact we've had on each other. This impact at times might be hidden and gets revealed sometimes even years later. The stories in this book will help you realize the power and influence we often wield without ever knowing it.

Written by most of the same authors as in earlier Spotlight series books with some new faces, we hope this book will help you recognize significance in your own lives.

Spotlight on the Art of Fear

This seems unusual for a book title. How could there be an "Art" to fear? The stories covered in this book focus on the sources of our fears, how to face them and overcome them. Sometimes we must seek fearful situations in order for us to grow, to voluntarily go where we've never been before. The authors of this book have many unique perspectives that may strike a chord in your experiences. Read, absorb and apply this Art of Fear!

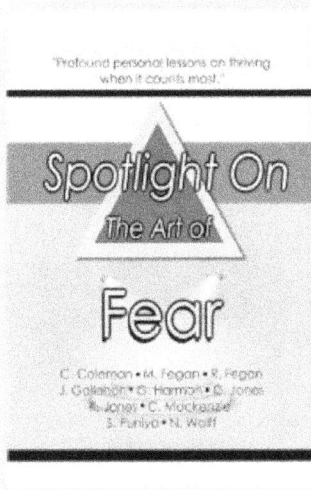

Spotlight on the Art of Generating Energy

Have you ever been in a room where the air crackled with excitement and creative thoughts? Do you know someone that brings positive energy to any situation? Have you ever wondered what makes some groups click and get monumental tasks done with ease? Our authors explore the energy-generating clues for the best results personally and in a group. Read this and charge yourself up!

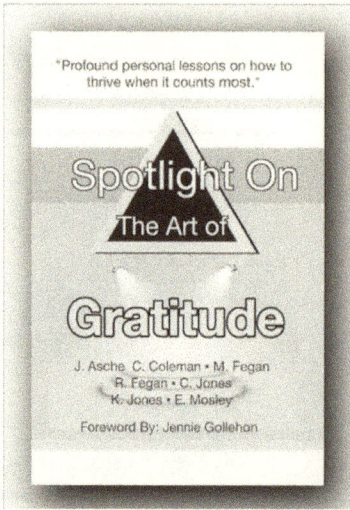

Spotlight on the Art of Gratitude

Do you have a mind and heart filled with gratitude? Are challenging times making it difficult for you to be grateful? How do you cope with times of isolation? How do you continue to feel gratitude in your life when facing challenges? This book provides answers to these and other questions.

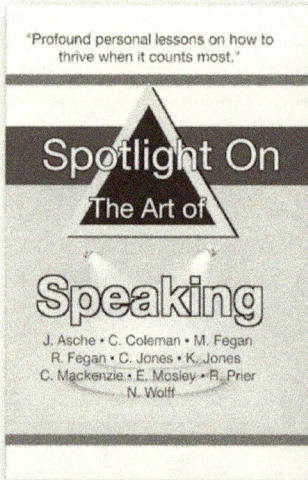

Spotlight on the Art of Speaking

Whether you are making a phone call or speaking to a group, we all speak. There may be times you struggle to find the words or you want to create a better speech. This compilation looks at many elements of how we speak. While many parts are serious, there is even room for humor.

Spotlight on the Art of Confidence

Confidence is an attitude that enables you to attempt new things during your life's journey. At times, you encounter situations that are new or challenging. Your confidence may falter or elude you. In this compilation, the authors share their insights on gaining, building and utilizing confidence.

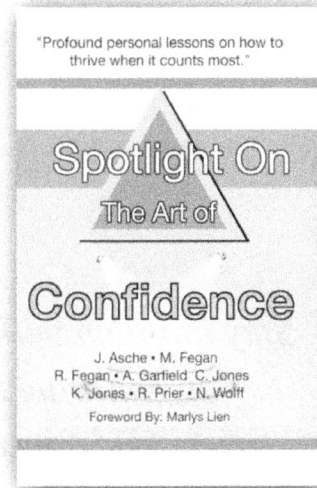

"Profound personal lessons on how to thrive when it counts most."

Spotlight On
The Art of
Confidence

J. Asche • M. Fegan
R. Fegan • A. Garfield C. Jones
K. Jones • R. Prier • N. Wolff
Foreword By: Marlys Lien

Spotlight on the Art of The Story

Stories capture our interest more easily than a dry recitation of facts. They bring to life experiences the teller wants to share, evoke empathy for the characters, and humanize the situations portrayed. In this compilation, the authors share their insights on how best to bring the stories within you to life.

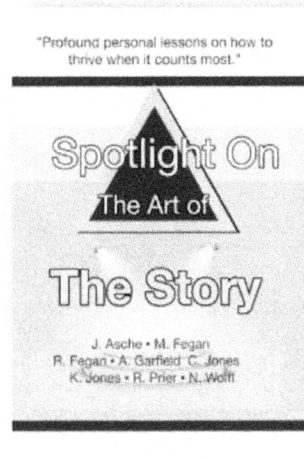

"Profound personal lessons on how to thrive when it counts most."

Spotlight On
The Art of
The Story

J. Asche • M. Fegan
R. Fegan • A. Garfield C. Jones
K. Jones • R. Prier • N. Wolff

Stay in touch with the Alternative Book Club as you continue to strive toward your goals, overcome adversity, and find your voice.

http://www.AlternativeBookClub.com

www.ingramcontent.com/pod-product-compliance
Lightning Source LLC
Chambersburg PA
CBHW031247090426
42742CB00007B/341